Canadian Living

GLORIOUS CHRISTMAS C·R·A·F·T·S

Canadian Living

GLORIOUS
CHRISTMAS
C·R·A·F·T·S

*A Treasury of Wonderful Creations
for the Holiday Season*
by Anna Hobbs and the craft editors
of *Canadian Living* Magazine

A CANADIAN LIVING/MADISON PRESS BOOK

Telemedia Publishing Inc.
50 Holly Street
Toronto, Ontario
Canada
M4S 3B3

Canadian Cataloguing in Publication Data
Main entry under title:
Glorious Christmas crafts
Includes index.
ISBN 0-394-22052-8
1. Christmas decorations.   2. Handicraft.
I. Hobbs, Anna.   II. Title: Canadian living.
TT900.C4H62 1988   745.594'1   C88-093067-5

Produced by
Madison Press Books
40 Madison Avenue
Toronto, Ontario
Canada
M5R 2S1

Printed in Italy

CONTENTS

INTRODUCTION

Christmas is a glorious season — a time when smiles are warmest, people, friendliest and children, wide-eyed with anticipation, capture our hearts. It's a time of treasured memories and fond anticipations, when every year holds the promise of being "the best Christmas ever."

Whatever the ingredients that make the season memorable for you — family, friends, faith, goodwill, music, grandma's cooking, laughter and, of course, lots of surprises — at the heart of Christmas are love and joy.

This book was written for those who love Christmas and have discovered the special joy in adding their own personal touch to holiday preparations and gifts. There are 152 pages jam-packed with imaginative ideas for decorating your home and trimming your tree; for making the gift you can hardly wait to give; planning a bang-up bazaar; and keeping little hands out of mischief at the busiest time of the year.

From beginner to expert, there's something here for everyone — from jolly paper Santas that can be turned out in minutes by the kindergarten crowd to a breathtaking treetop angel to inspire an experienced needleworker. You'll find adorable dolls and toys to light up the faces of small members of the family — as well as things they can make, too. Many of the ideas here are more-love-than-money crafts made with materials you already have around the house. There are projects to embroider, knit, stitch, quilt, cut and paste, carve from wood and paint. Some need to be kept a secret while hidden under construction for weeks. Others can be whipped up at a moment's notice.

Full-color photographs accompany each project. The instructions are written in an easy-to-follow, step-by-step format with a complete list of supplies needed. Thanks to the care and attention to detail of Jean Scobie, assistant craft editor of *Canadian Living*, you will find these instructions concise yet detailed enough to leave no unanswered questions. Eighteen patterns are full size and ready to duplicate immediately. Patterns for larger projects are shown on a grid which can be scaled up to size, easily and accurately.

Many people have made this book possible. They are the artists, craftspeople, designers and teachers who have discovered the joy in working with their hands and to whom adding their own loving touches to Christmas is important. Their names accompany each project. Most of these projects have appeared in *Canadian Living* magazine and in *Canadian Living's Christmas Idea Book*. Some are brand new. All were chosen with a view to help you create a memorable Christmas.

Selecting the best ideas from twelve years of magazines and deciding which irresistible new items to add is a mammoth assignment. Compiling a project from here and a design from there and seeing them come to life in the pages of this book has equalled the excitement of a wide-eyed child on Christmas morning. That special Christmas thrill has been a year-long event. May you have as much fun with these ideas as we have. Enjoy the season and have the most glorious Christmas ever!

— Anna Hobbs

Canadian Living

GLORIOUS CHRISTMAS CRAFTS

CHRISTMAS ALL THROUGH THE HOUSE

CHAPTER I

A COUNTRY CHRISTMAS

Savor the simple joys of an old-fashioned Christmas with fun and folksy decorating ideas. A century-old, lovingly restored farmhouse filled with innovative holiday crafts provides inspiration for any decor. There's a charming wooden village to adorn a mantel or tabletop, perky papier-mâché birds and wonderful wooden reindeer. Each decoration is guaranteed to be an absorbing project for the entire family. Complete the country theme with table linens and accessories, a pretty little doll and a Starry Night Stocking.

WOODEN VILLAGE

Design by Jane Buckles

YOU NEED:
- Softwood, such as knot-free pine, 1 piece 2 in × 6 in × 8 ft, for buildings,* and 1 piece 1 × 8 × 34 in, for trees and mill wheel
- 3/8- × 3/4-in balsa wood strip, 30 in long
- Scraps of 1/4-in dowelling, for lightning rod and barber pole
- 2-1/2-in and 1-1/4-in spiral nails
- White craft glue
- Sandpaper
- X-acto knife
- Saw and jigsaw
- Hammer
- Vise
- Gesso or wood primer
- Acrylic paint in assorted colors
- Artist's paintbrushes
- Pencil with new eraser on end
- Spray varnish
- *At lumberyard or where an electric

tablesaw is available, cut this piece into 33-in and 63-in lengths. On 33-in length, cut off one long edge at a 60° angle as shown in Diagram 1. On 63-in length, cut off one long edge at a 45° angle as shown in Diagram 2.

TO MAKE:

Note: Sand all edges of wooden blocks as they are cut. Refer to diagrams as you proceed.

HOUSES A AND F, SHOPS B AND C
From angled 33-in length of pine, cut off:
- two 5-1/2-in lengths, for house A
- two 4-in lengths, for house F
- four 3-1/2-in lengths, for shops B and C

Glue and nail pieces of same size together in pairs in shape of basic building shown in Diagram 3.

SHOP D, HOUSE E, CHURCH, BARN AND MILL
From angled 63-in length of pine, cut off:
- one 6-1/2-in length, for shop D

- one 25-in length, for house E and church
- two 5-3/4-in lengths, for barn
- three 4-1/2-in lengths, for mill
- one 3-1/2-in length, for mill

1. **Shop D:** Cut 1-1/4 in off long unangled bottom edge of 6-1/2-in length (see Diagram 4). Set scrap aside for church. Cut piece in half vertically so you have two 3-1/4-in lengths. Glue and nail these 2 pieces together in shape of basic building shown in Diagram 3.

2. **House E:** Cut 3/4 in off long unangled bottom edge of 25-in length (see Diagram 5). Discard scrap. Cut piece vertically into five 5-in lengths. Set aside 2 of these pieces for church. Glue and nail 2 pieces together in shape of basic building shown in Diagram 3. Cut 1-1/4 in off unangled bottom edge of remaining piece, then cut in half vertically as shown in Diagram 6. Discard shaded parts. Glue and nail remaining part onto side of house to form porch (Diagram 7).

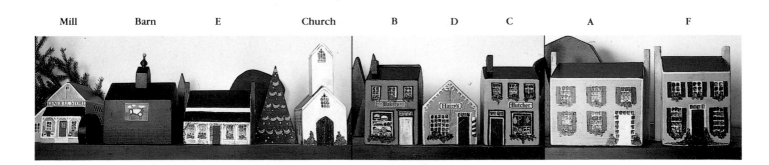

Mill   Barn   E   Church   B   D   C   A   F

WOODEN VILLAGE

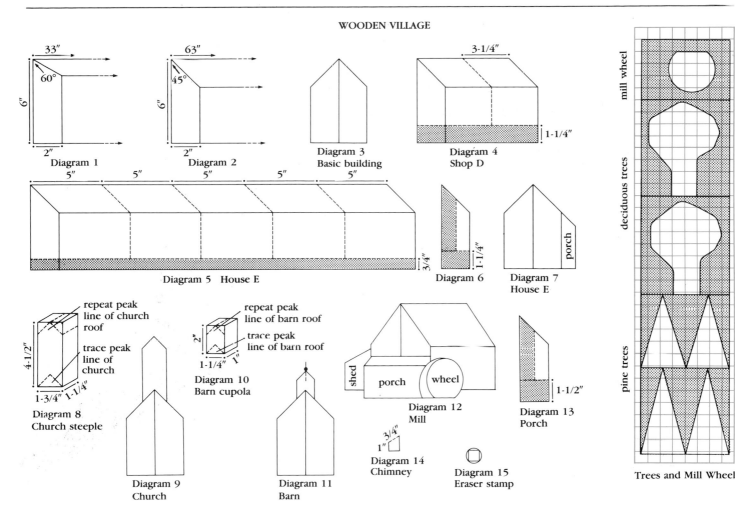

Diagram 1

Diagram 2

Diagram 3
Basic building

Diagram 4
Shop D

Diagram 5   House E

Diagram 6

Diagram 7
House E

Diagram 8
Church steeple

Diagram 9
Church

Diagram 10
Barn cupola

Diagram 11
Barn

Diagram 12
Mill

Diagram 13
Porch

Diagram 14
Chimney

Diagram 15
Eraser stamp

Trees and Mill Wheel

mill wheel

deciduous trees

pine trees

3. **Church:** Glue and nail together two 5-in pieces set aside in Step 2 in shape of basic building shown in Diagram 3. From 1-1/4-in scrap saved from shop D, cut a 4-1/2-in length, to make a block 1-1/4 × 1-3/4 × 4-1/2 in. Measure and mark cutting lines on block shown in Diagram 8. Cut along dotted lines to form church steeple. Glue steeple in place on top of one end of church (Diagram 9).

4. **Barn:** Glue and nail two 5-3/4-lengths together in shape of basic building shown in Diagram 3. From scrap, cut a 1- × 1-1/4- × 2-in block for cupola. Measure and mark cutting lines on block shown in Diagram 10. Cut along dotted lines. Glue cupola in place on centre of barn roof. Drill a 1/4-in diameter hole in centre top of cupola. Glue and insert a 1-3/4-in length of dowelling (threaded with bead if desired) in hole to form lightning rod (Diagram 11).

5. **Mill:** Glue and nail two 4-1/2-in lengths together in shape of basic building shown

in Diagram 3. For shed, cut 2 in. off unangled bottom edge of remaining 4-1/2-in length. Glue and nail onto side of mill (Diagram 12). For front porch, cut 1-1/2 in off unangled bottom edge of 3-1/2-in length, then cut in half vertically as shown in Diagram 13. Discard shaded parts. Glue and nail remaining part onto front end of mill to form porch (Diagram 12). Mill wheel will be cut later.

TREES AND MILL WHEEL
Enlarge patterns for trees and mill wheel by the squaring method (see General Directions, page 134) directly onto 1- × 8- × 34-in pine instead of brown paper. Cut out pieces with saw and jigsaw. Glue mill wheel onto side of mill (Diagram 12).

TO FINISH:
Sand all pieces thoroughly.

1. **House A:** With small handsaw, cut two 5-3/4-in lengths of balsa wood. Glue 1 strip to each end of house for chimneys.

2. **Shops B and C:** Cut four 1-in lengths of balsa wood for chimneys. Cut bottom edge of each chimney at an angle to correspond to angle of roof (Diagram 14). Glue chimneys in place.

3. **Houses E and F:** Cut two 5-1/2-in lengths from the balsa wood. Glue 1 strip to the end of each house for the chimneys.

TO PAINT:
Paint your village as desired. Ours has been painted to depict the summer season on one side of each building and the Christmas season on the other. Trees show summer leaves on one side and bare winter branches on the other. Refer to photo for suggested colors and designs. Here are a few painting tips:

1. Paint all parts with gesso or a similar primer paint.

2. Work from large to small, allowing paint to dry before applying next color. First paint the walls and roof, then

A novel tree trim, Twig Reindeer (above) can be adapted to serve as a table decoration (opposite page) by adding a base and wheels.

window and door shapes, then, shutters, door frames and trim lines, and finally the small decorative details such as flowers in window boxes, wreaths, baked goods in bakery window, barber pole, snow, etc.

3. **Window panes:** With X-acto knife, cut eraser on end of pencil into a rectangle (Diagram 15). Use this to stamp panes on windows and around doors.

4. **Signs:** Letraset sign names on paper, cut out and glue onto buildings with white craft glue. Paint glue over sign to seal.

5. Allow paint to dry thoroughly. Spray-varnish all buildings.

TWIG REINDEER

Design by Jane Buckles

Larger reindeer on wheels stands 23 cm (9 in) high. Smaller reindeer suitable for tree decoration measures 18 cm (7 in) high.

YOU NEED:

For larger reindeer:
- **Logs with or without bark, preferably a softwood such as pine or cedar in the following dimensions:**
  - **1-1/2-in diameter cut into 1 piece 2-1/2-in long, for head, and 4 pieces 1/2-in long, for wheels**
  - **2-1/2-in diameter, 5 to 6 in long, for body**
- **Dowelling in the following dimensions:**
  - **4 pieces, 1/2-in diameter each 5-3/4-in long, for legs**
  - **1 piece, 3/4-in diameter, 1-1/2-in long, for neck**
  - **2 pieces, 1/4-in diameter, each 1-1/4-in long, for ears OR two 1/4-in dowel pins (available at lumber or hardward stores)**
  - **5 pieces, 3/8-in diameter, each 1-1/4 in long for tail and axles OR five 3/8-in dowel pins**
  - **4 pieces, 1/8-in diameter, each 1 in long, for axle pins**
- **Scrap of pine, 1 × 3 × 4-1/2 in, for base**
- **2 antler-shaped branches (apple tree branches and twigs work well)**
- **2 wooden hole plugs, 3/8-in diameter,**

for eyes (available at most lumber and hardware stores)
For smaller reindeer:
- **Logs as described above in the following dimension:**
  - **1-3/4-in diameter, 3 in long, for body**
  - **1-1/4-in diameter, 1-3/4 in long, for head**
- **Dowelling in the following dimensions:**
  - **4 pieces, 3/8-in diameter, each 3 in long, for legs**
  - **1 piece, 3/8-in diameter, 1-1/2 in long, for neck**

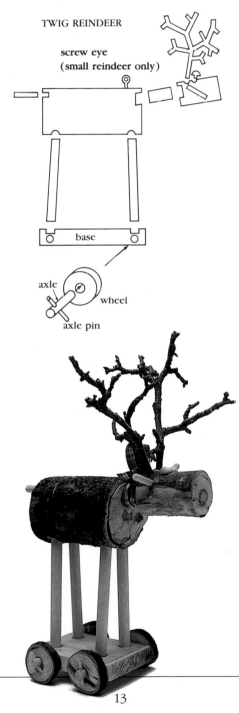

TWIG REINDEER

screw eye
(small reindeer only)

base

axle

wheel

axle pin

- **Three 1/4-in dowel pins, for ears and tail**
- **2 small wooden hole plugs, 1/4-in diameter, for eyes**
- **2 small antler-shaped branches, for antlers**
- **1 small screw eye**
For both projects:
- **Electric drill with assortment of bits to correspond to diameter of dowelling and branches**
- **Saw**
- **Glue gun and glue sticks or white craft glue**

TO MAKE:

Note: Refer to diagrams as you proceed.

1. In one end of head and one end of body, drill holes 3/4 in deep for large reindeer, or 1/2 in deep for smaller reindeer. Glue and insert neck dowelling into holes to join head to body.

2. Drill 2 holes for ears on either side of head, 2 holes for eyes in top of head and 1 hole for tail in tail end. Glue and insert appropriate dowel pins.

3. Drill 4 holes for legs in bottom of body. Glue and insert legs.

4. Drill 2 holes for antler branches on top of head behind eyes. Glue and insert antler branches.

5. Tie decorative ribbon or bell around neck or antlers, if desired. For smaller reindeer tree decoration, screw eye into top of body close to head and attach a hanging thread.

For larger reindeer only, proceed as follows:

6. Stand reindeer on base and mark positions for 4 leg holes. Drill holes 1/4 in deep. With 3/8-in drill bit and clamping wood in vice if necessary, carefully drill 2 holes in each side of base under each leg.

7. With 1/2-in drill bit, drill a hole all the way through centre of each log wheel. With 1/8-in drill bit, drill hole near one end of each axle, all the way through.

8. To assemble, insert 1/8-in axle pins through hole in end of each axle. Insert axles through wheels and glue into holes on sides of base. Glue and insert legs into holes in top of base.

Brown Bag Buildings are an innovative (and economical) way to wrap and decorate presents. Or use scraps of fabric to make simple Fabric Sacks.

BROWN BAG BUILDINGS

Design by Jo Calvert

YOU NEED:

- **Plain brown bags with flat bottoms**
- **Black construction paper**
- **Felt-tip markers in assorted colors**
- **Scraps of ribbon**
- **Scraps of lightweight cardboard (optional)**
- **Scissors**
- **Ruler**
- **Hole punch**

TO MAKE:

1. With markers, draw simple shapes for door, windows, shutters, etc., on front and back of flat bag, referring to photo (this page) if desired. Open bag and place upright. If desired, stiffen bottom of bag by measuring bottom, then cutting and fitting a piece of cardboard inside.

2. Place gift in bag. Fold down top of bag. For roof; cut a piece of black paper the width of front of bag. Fold paper in half parallel to width, and place over top of bag. Trim away excess paper so roof is desired height. Punch holes through all layers approx 2 cm (3/4 in) below fold. Thread ribbons through holes and tie to close.

FABRIC SACKS

Design by Jo Calvert

YOU NEED:

- **Scraps of printed or plain cotton fabric**
- **Scraps of ribbon**
- **Ruler**
- **Matching thread**

TO MAKE:

1. From fabric, cut a pair of rectangular, square or stocking shapes slightly larger than desired finished size. Press under 6 mm (1/4 in), then 6 mm again, along 1 edge (top edge) of each piece. Stitch.

2. From contrasting colored fabric, cut 2 casing strips. Each strip should be 2 cm

(3/4 in) shorter than width of top edge and 3 cm (1-1/8 in) wider than ribbon. Press under 1 cm (3/8 in) along all casing strip edges. On right side, centre each strip parallel to and approx 4 cm (1-5/8 in) from top edges. Edgestitch in place along long edges.

3. If desired, machine-appliqué initial or name to 1 fabric piece. With right sides together, stitch, using a 1 cm seam allowance and leaving top edge open. Clip corners or curves. Bind raw edges of seam allowance with zigzag stitching, if desired. Turn sack right side out.

4. Thread ribbon through each casing. Pull up tightly and tie a bow at each side of bag.

BIRD ON A SWING

Design by Jane Buckles

YOU NEED:

- **Styrofoam egg, 10 × 7.5 cm (4 × 3 in)**
- **Coat hanger wire, one 35.5 cm (14-in) length and four 9 cm (3-1/2-in) lengths**
- **1/2-in dowelling, 1 piece 4-1/2 in long and 1 piece 1 in long**
- **2 wooden beads, 8 mm in diameter, for eyes**
- **1 small feather**
- **.20 m factory cotton (unbleached muslin)**
- **Newspaper**
- **Wallpaper paste**
- **Glue gun and glue sticks (optional)**
- **White craft glue**
- **Gesso**
- **Acrylic paint in assorted colors**
- **Artist's paintbrushes**
- **Spray varnish**
- **Saw**
- **Pliers**
- **Wire cutter**
- **Scissors**
- **File or sandpaper**
- **Electric drill with bit to correspond to diameter of wire**

TO MAKE:

1. **Perch:** Bend 35.5 cm length of wire in half, then, using pliers, shape each half into perch as shown in Diagram 1. Drill

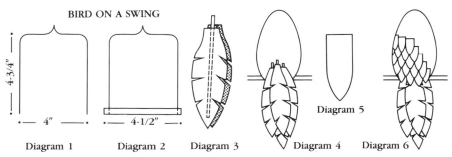

BIRD ON A SWING

4-3/4"

4"

4-1/2"

Diagram 1   Diagram 2   Diagram 3   Diagram 5   Diagram 4   Diagram 6

a hole 1/4 in from each end of 4-1/2-in length of dowelling to fit wire. Insert and glue ends of wire in holes (see Diagram 2). With small end up, position Styrofoam egg on perch and with a knife, carve a narrow groove in the underside of egg to accommodate perch. Egg will be glued to perch along this groove later.

2. **Beak:** Sand or file one end of 1-in length of dowelling into a dull point. Push opposite end into head at beak level and glue in place.

3. **Body:** Mix up approx 1 cup (250 mL) wallpaper paste to ketchup-like consistency. Add about 1/4 cup (50 mL) white craft glue. Tear newspaper into 4 × 2.5 cm (1-1/2- × 1-in) pieces. Smear egg with lots of paste and glue on one layer of newspaper pieces, overlapping pieces generously as you go, leaving beak uncovered and retaining groove for perch. Set aside to dry thoroughly. Glue bird to perch.

4. **Tail feathers:** From muslin, cut 8 tail

feathers approx 7.5 × 2.5 (3 × 1 in) as shown in Diagram 3. Clip sides as shown. Soak all feathers in paste. Glue feathers together in pairs, sandwiching a 9 cm length of wire between each pair (end of wire should extend beyond base of feathers). Push each tail feather into tail end of bird as shown in Diagram 4.

5. **Feathers:** From muslin, cut 50 to 60 small feathers approx 4 × 1.5 cm (1-1/2 × 5/8 in) and tiny feathers approx 6 mm × 2.5 cm (1/4 × 1 in) as shown in Diagram 5. Soak all feathers in paste. Starting at tail end of bird, glue feathers to body in overlapping rows around base of tail and entire body up to head (Diagram 6). Glue tiny feathers to head in overlapping rows radiating out from beak. Hang to dry.

6. Glue on eyes. Paint perch desired color. Let dry.

7. Paint bird with gesso. Let dry. Paint bird in desired colors. Refer to photo for suggested colors and designs. Paint beak and eyes. When dry, spray varnish.

8. Poke a small hole in top of head. Insert and glue feather in place.

REINDEER WALL PLAQUE

Design by Jane Buckles

YOU NEED:
- **1 log as described for twig reindeer, (page 13) 2-1/2-in diameter, 5 in long, for head/neck**
- **Two 3/8-in dowel pins, for ears**
- **2 wooden hole plugs, 3/8-in diameter, for eyes (available at most lumber and hardware stores)**
- **Scrap of pine, 1 × 5-1/2 × 6 in, for plaque**
- **2 antler-shaped branches**
- **1 small screw eye**
- **2 screws, 2-1/2 in long**
- **Electric drill with 3/8-in bit, inset bit and bit to correspond to size of screws**
- **Saw**
- **Glue gun and glue sticks or white craft glue**

TO MAKE:
Note: Refer to diagrams as you proceed.

Papier-mâché Bird On A Swing.

Similar to Twig Reindeer only larger, Reindeer Wall Plaque becomes a conversation piece when hung on a wall or door.

REINDEER WALL PLAQUE

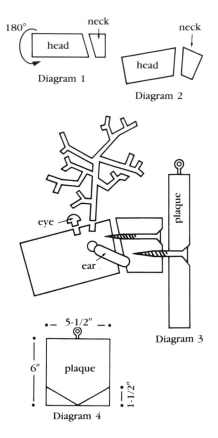

1. Cut log at a very slight angle as shown in Diagram 1. Turn longer end of log (head) around 180° so it is at an angle to

the shorter piece (neck) as shown in Diagram 2.

2. With neck and head pieces held together, drill hole through neck into head using a drill bit same size as screw (see Diagram 3). Glue and screw neck to head. Insert screw so it does not stick out at back of neck.

3. Cut angles at one end of plaque as shown in Diagram 4. Screw eye into centre of top edge.

4. Position head/neck on plaque slightly below centre. Drill hole through back of plaque into neck. Glue and screw plaque to head/neck. Inset screw.

5. Drill 2 holes for ears in side of head, 2 holes for eyes in top of head and 2 holes for antler branches behind eyes. Glue all parts in place.

6. Tie decorative ribbon or bell around neck or antlers, if desired.

SIMPLE STRIP PATCHWORK

Design by Jo Calvert

GENERAL DIRECTIONS
YOU NEED:
- **Short lengths or scraps of printed or plain cottons**
- **Matching thread**
- **Dressmaker's chalk pencil**
- **Metre stick**

TO MAKE PATCHWORK PIECES:
Patchwork is made up of fabric strips of various widths cut on straight grain and sewn together into one piece. Length and number of strips necessary are determined by size of patchwork piece needed for each project. Refer to specific instructions for required sizes.

1. Press all fabric. Using metre stick and chalk pencil, measure, mark and accurately cut strips of desired width and length on crosswise or lengthwise straight grain of fabric. Remember to include extra width for seam allowances.

2. Select a centre strip. You may wish to choose a color that matches backing/border fabric. Arrange remaining strips as desired on either side of centre strip so that design is symmetrical.

3. With right sides together and using a closely spaced machine stitch, sew one long edge of centre strip and one long edge of adjoining right-hand strip together. Sew other long edge of centre strip to adjoining left-hand strip in same manner. Continue sewing adjoining strips together, alternating from right- to left-hand side to prevent curling.

PLACE MAT AND NAPKIN

Design by Jo Calvert

Finished place mat measures 45 × 32 cm (17-3/4 × 12-5/8 in).

YOU NEED:
For 1 place mat and napkin:
- **Piece of patchwork (having strips parallel to long edges), 45 × 32 cm (17-3/4 × 12-5/8 in)**
- **Piece of printed or plain cotton, 54 × 41 cm (21-1/4 × 16-1/8 in), for backing**
- **Piece of printed or plain cotton, 40 cm (15-3/4 in) square, for napkin**
- **Piece of polyester batting, 45 × 32 cm**
- **Thread to match backing**
- **Dressmaker's chalk pencil**
- **Ruler**

TO MAKE:
Note: For a neat finish to quilting lines, pull thread ends through to back of work. Knot ends close to fabric, two at a time, then thread back between fabric layers for approx 2 cm (3/4 in) and out again. Clip.

1. On right side of patchwork, measure and mark a chalk line 1.5 cm (5/8 in) in from each raw edge.

2. Lay backing wrong side up on a flat working surface; centre batting on top then centre patchwork, right side up, on top of batting. Baste around edges through all layers.

3. Pin patchwork to backing every 5 cm (2 in) along edges of strips with pins at right angles to long edges to prevent fabric from shifting as you quilt. Working from centre strip outward, machine-quilt by edgestitching long edges of each strip from chalk line to chalk line.

4. Lay mat, backing side up. Press under

*The table linens, apron and pot holder are made using a simple strip patchwork method.
Patchwork, Place Mat and Napkin instructions begin on p. 16. Instructions for Table Runner,
Hot Mat, Pot Holder, Bun Basket Napkin and Apron follow on pp. 18 and 19.*

1.5 cm along all edges. Turn mat over, patchwork side up. To form border, wrap backing around each short edge of mat so folded edge meets chalk line. Pin. Wrap backing around long edges in same manner so long borders overlap short borders neatly at corners. Pin. Slipstitch overlaps at corners. Edgestitch inner and outer edges of border around mat. Remove basting.

5. To make napkin, turn under 6 mm (1/4 in), then 6 mm again around all edges. Stitch.

TABLE RUNNER

Design by Jo Calvert

Finished runner measures 178 × 32 cm (70-1/8 × 12-5/8 in). You may wish to adjust length for size of your table.

YOU NEED:
- **Piece of patchwork, 32 cm (12-5/8 in) square**
- **2 pieces of patchwork (having strips parallel to long edges), each 75 × 32 cm (29-1/2 × 12-5/8 in)**
- **Piece of plain or printed cotton, 187 × 41 cm (73-7/8 × 16-1/8 in), for backing**
- **Piece of polyester batting, 178 × 32 cm**
- **Thread to match backing**
- **Dressmaker's chalk pencil**
- **Ruler**

TO MAKE:

1. With right sides together, stitch patchwork square to one short end of 1 patchwork rectangle, so that strips run at right angles to each other. With right sides together, stitch one short end of remaining patchwork rectangle to opposite edge of square. Press seams open.

2. Read Note and follow Steps 1 and 2 of place mat instructions.

3. Pin patchwork to backing every 5 cm (2 in) along edges of strips with pins at right angles to long edges to prevent fabric from shifting as you quilt. Machine-quilt centre patchwork square as for place mat, working from centre strip outward. Machine-quilt patchwork

rectangles from edge of square to chalk line in same manner.

4. Make borders as for place mat, Step 4.

HOT MAT

Design by Jo Calvert

Finished hot mat measures 32 cm (12-5/8 in) square.

YOU NEED:
- **Piece of patchwork 32 cm square**
- **Piece of printed or plain cotton, 41 cm (16-1/8 in) square, for backing**
- **Piece of thermal interlining (compressed batting with shiny foil on one side), 32 cm square**
- **Thread to match backing**
- **Dressmaker's chalk pencil**
- **Ruler**

TO MAKE:
Follow Steps 1 to 4 of place mat instructions, being sure to have shiny side of thermal batting facing *up* in Step 2.

POT HOLDER

Design by Jo Calvert

Finished pot holder measures 23 cm (9 in) square.

YOU NEED:
- **Piece of patchwork, 23 cm square**
- **Piece of printed or plain cotton, 23 cm square, for backing**
- **Piece of thermal interlining (compressed batting with shiny foil on one side), 23 cm square**
- **1.10 m printed or plain wide double-fold bias tape**
- **Thread to match backing**
- **Ruler**

TO MAKE:

1. Follow Steps 1 to 3 of place mat instructions, being sure to have shiny side of thermal batting facing *down* in Step 2. When quilting is complete slightly round all corners with scissors.

2. Cut a 14 cm (5-1/2-in) length of bias tape. Stitch long folded edges together. To make a loop, fold in half so short ends meet. Pin loop to right side of pot holder at one corner, having raw edges of loop and pot holder even. Cut a 95 cm (37-3/8-in) length of bias tape. Pin around pot holder, enclosing raw edges in fold. Stitch. Fold loop away from pot holder, and zigzag across bottom edge. Remove basting.

BUN BASKET NAPKIN

Design by Jo Calvert

Finished napkin is 53 cm (20-7/8 in) square.

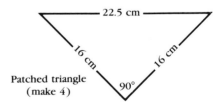

Patched triangle (make 4) | 22.5 cm | 16 cm | 16 cm | 90°

YOU NEED:
- **4 patched triangles, each with one long edge of 22.5 cm (8-3/4 in) having patched strips parallel to long edge, and two short edges of 16 cm (6-1/4 in), having a right angle at their junction (see Diagram above)**
- **2 pieces of printed or plain cotton, each 55 cm (21-5/8 in) square**
- **Thread to match cotton squares**
- **Dressmaker's chalk pencil**
- **Ruler**

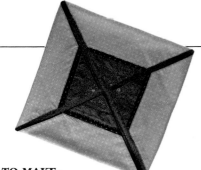

TO MAKE:

1. Lay 1 cotton square, right side up, on a flat working surface. From each corner, measure 13 cm (5-1/8 in) along edge in each direction and mark with chalk pencil. Draw a straight line across each corner from one marked point to the other. Cut off corners along drawn lines. With right sides together and long edge of each triangle even with and centred over each cut edge at corners, stitch 4 triangles in place using a 1 cm (3/8-in) seam allowance. Press seams open.

2. With right sides together, stitch patched square to remaining cotton square, using a 1 cm seam allowance and leaving open along one edge. Clip corners. Turn right side out. Press under 1 cm around opening. Pin together. Press other edges flat. Edgestitch all edges of napkin. Machine-quilt corners by edgestitching strips.

PATCHWORK APRON

Design by Jo Calvert

YOU NEED:
- **Piece of patchwork (having strips parallel to long edges), 82 × 24 cm (32-1/4 × 9-1/2 in)**
- **1.30 m printed or plain cotton, 115 cm wide**
- **Matching thread**
- **Ruler**
- **Brown paper**

TO MAKE:

To enlarge pattern, see General Directions (page 134).

1. From cotton, cut apron, 1 strip 55 × 7 cm (21-5/8 × 2-3/4 in), 2 strips each 80 × 7 cm (31-1/2 × 2-3/4 in), and 1 rectangle 82 × 24 cm.

2. Clip curved side edges of apron, turn under 6 mm (1/4 in), then 6 mm again. Topstitch. Hem remaining side, top and bottom edges in same manner.

3. **Neck loop:** Press under 1 cm (3/8 in) along both long edges of short strip. Fold in half so folded edges meet. Pin. Edgestitch all edges. Press under 6 mm at both ends. Pin ends to top corners of apron indicated by Xs. Topstitch in place along dotted lines.

4. **Waist ties:** Press under 1 cm along both long edges and one short end of each long strip. Fold in half so folded edges meet. Pin. Edgestitch all edges. Press under 6 mm at remaining raw end, then pin to apron at each side corner indicated by Xs. Topstitch ties in place along dotted lines.

5. **Pocket:** With right sides together and using a 1 cm seam allowance, stitch patchwork rectangle to cotton rectangle, leaving open along one short edge. Clip corners. Turn right side out. Press under 1 cm around opening. Slipstitch opening closed. Press. Edgestitch one long edge (top edge).

6. Pin and machine-quilt patchwork pocket as for place mat, Step 3.

7. Lay quilted patchwork pocket, right side up, on front of apron, so bottom and side edges are even. Pin. Edgestitch pocket to apron along bottom and side edges. Divide pocket into 4 equal segments with vertical rows of stitching.

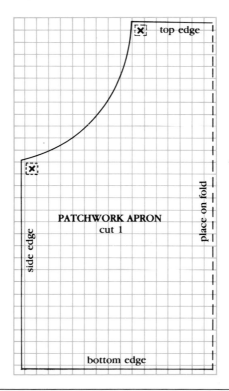

PATCHWORK APRON
cut 1

side edge

place on fold

top edge

bottom edge

STARRY NIGHT STOCKING

Design by Jo Calvert

YOU NEED:
- **.50 m red calico, 115 cm wide, for lining, binding and ties**
- **.50 m unbleached muslin, 115 cm wide, for interlining**
- **Piece of blue calico, 50 × 30 cm (19-3/4 × 11-7/8 in), for sky**
- **Scraps of solid color and printed cotton in assorted colors, white and natural, for appliqué**
- **2 pieces of polyester batting, each 50 × 40 cm (19-3/4 × 15-3/4 in)**
- **Small gold sequin stars**
- **Matching thread**
- **Dressmaker's chalk pencil**
- **Brown paper**

TO MAKE:

To enlarge pattern, see General Directions (page 134).

Note: A 1 cm (3/8-in) seam allowance is included along *outside edges of stocking only*. Solid lines indicate cutting lines for paper pattern. Dotted lines indicate decorative stitching lines.

1. From brown paper, cut out patterns for main stocking shapes along outer edges (bold lines) only. From batting, muslin and red calico, cut stocking front and back. From red calico, cut 3 strips 50 × 5.5 cm (19-3/4 × 2-1/8 in). Set aside.

2. Cut paper pattern along inner (thin) solid lines. Lay all pattern pieces on right side of appropriate colored fabric (see color labels on pattern). With dressmaker's chalk pencil, trace around each pattern piece, leaving at least 1.5 cm (5/8 in) between pieces on same fabric.

3. Cut fabric as follows: Along underlap edges (indicated by small arrows), cut 6 mm (1/4 in) out from traced lines for underlap allowance. Along remaining overlap and outside edges, cut along traced lines.

4. Assemble stocking front and back, matching cut edges of overlaps with chalk lines on underlaps. Baste. With wrong sides together, baste one muslin stocking to stocking front, then the other to stocking back, along outside edges. Using

matching thread and a wide, closely spaced zigzag stitch, appliqué pieces together. Stitch decorative stitching lines as indicated. To finish each stitching line neatly, pull threads to wrong side. Knot close to fabric and clip.

5. Sandwich 1 batting stocking between wrong sides of stocking front and lining. Baste together around outside edges. Using white thread and straight stitch, machine-quilt around outline of appliqué shapes and along horizontal lines in sky indicated by broken lines. Repeat for stocking back.

6. With right sides together and using a

1 cm seam allowance, stitch stocking front to back, leaving top edge open. Clip curves. Trim seam allowance to 6 mm. Bind raw edges of seam allowance to 6 mm. Bind raw edges of seam allowance with zigzag stitch. Remove basting.

7. For stocking ties, press under 1 cm along two long edges and one short end of 2 red calico strips. Fold each in half so folded edges meet. Topstitch folded edges together. With raw ends of ties and top edge of stocking even, baste ties, one on top of another, at back seam.

8. For binding, press under 1 cm along one long edge and one short end of

remaining red calico strip. With right side of strip and wrong side of stocking together, pin unfolded long edge around top edge of stocking. Lap short raw end over folded end approx 6 mm and trim away excess binding. Stitch. Turn stocking right side out. Fold and pin binding over and down 1.5 cm from top edge of stocking. Edgestitch top and bottom of binding through all layers, catching tie ends in stitching. Fold ties upward and zigzag across bottom edge. Tie ends of ties into a bow.

9. Hand-stitch star sequins to sky as desired.

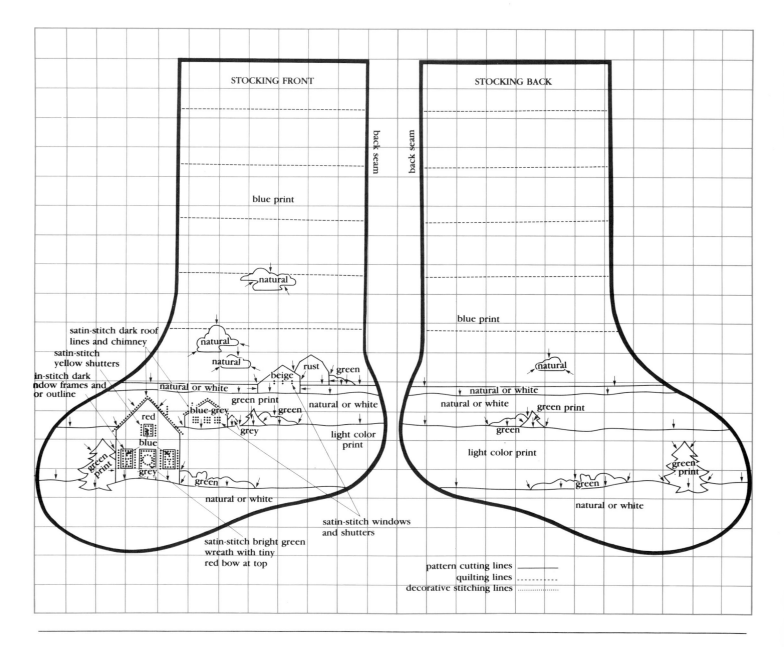

Hang a Starry Night Stocking by the banister and fill it with assorted surprises. Instructions begin on p. 19.

EMMA DOLL

Design by Judy Pilgrim Stewart

The finished doll is 38 cm (15 in) tall. It is hand washable. If pencilled features wash off, simply redraw them.

YOU NEED:
- .80 m unbleached muslin, 90 cm wide, for body and nightgown
- Piece of bright red calico, 44 cm (17-3/8 in) square, for dress
- 2 calico strips, 44 × 3 cm (17-3/8 × 1-1/8 in), in each of the following colors: navy, bright blue and rust, for dress patchwork
- Piece of bright blue calico, 40 × 20 cm (15-3/4 × 7-7/8 in), for pantaloons
- Piece of light-colored calico, 48 × 18 cm (18-7/8 × 7 in), for petticoat
- 1 m flat ecru cotton lace, 15 mm wide
- .30 m gathered ecru cotton lace, 15 mm wide
- .30 m red satin ribbon, 3 mm wide
- .40 m elastic, 10 mm wide
- Wool or mohair roving (or scraps of heavy yarn), for hair
- 4 snap fasteners, 6 mm in diameter
- Matching thread
- Polyester fibrefill
- Knitting needle
- Black acrylic paint
- Colored pencils
- Brown paper

TO MAKE:
To enlarge pattern, see General Directions (page 134).

Note: Use a 6 mm (1/4-in) seam allowance throughout, unless otherwise indicated. Sew body together using a closely spaced machine stitch. On all clothing, bind raw edges of seam allowances with machine zigzag.

1. **Body:** From muslin, cut 2 body pieces. With right sides together, machine-stitch body front to body back, leaving opening for stuffing at top of head. Clip curves. Turn right side out. Stuff with fibrefill, pushing stuffing into arms, legs and body with knitting needle. Slipstitch opening closed. Hand-stitch through body along broken lines indicated on pattern to form arm and leg joints. Paint black shoes. With red pencil, draw stocking stripes.

2. **Hair:** Using strong thread and small backstitches, sew roving to head, starting at base of neck. Work around head in a spiral fashion to centre back of head, covering head seam.

3. **Face:** Wet tips of sharpened colored pencils and draw face as follows: Make 2 circles for eyes in desired color. With black pencil draw pupils. With light brown pencil, draw half-circular inner eyelid lines, eyelid lines and eyebrows. With pink pencil, draw mouth, nostrils and small inner eye dot at edge of each pupil, then lightly draw rosy cheeks. Add a little red or deep pink to centre of mouth.

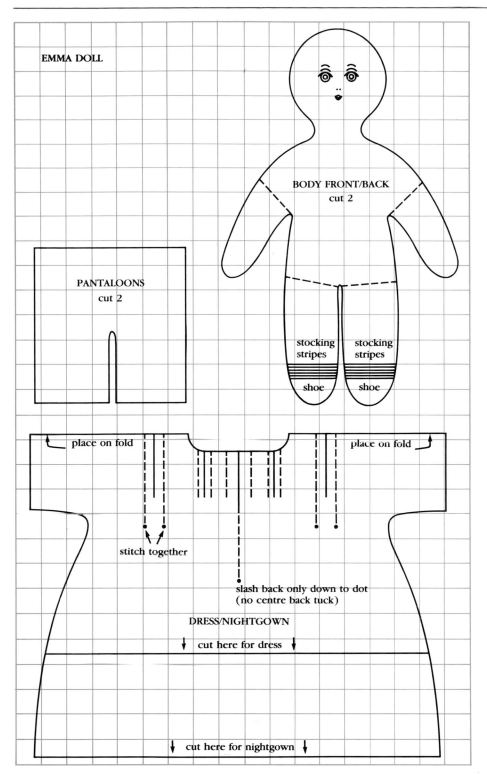

EMMA DOLL

BODY FRONT/BACK
cut 2

PANTALOONS
cut 2

stocking
stripes

stocking
stripes

shoe

shoe

place on fold

place on fold

stitch together

slash back only down to dot
(no centre back tuck)

DRESS/NIGHTGOWN

↓ cut here for dress ↓

↓ cut here for nightgown ↓

5. **Petticoat:** Turn under 6 mm, then 6 mm again along one long edge of petticoat calico. Hem. Fold in half so right sides are together and short edges meet. Stitch side seam. Around remaining raw edge, make a casing and insert elastic as for pantaloons.

6. **Dress:** From dress calico, cut 2 strips 44 × 5 cm (17-3/8 × 2 in). This leaves a rectangle 44 × 34 cm (17-3/8 × 13-1/2 in). With right sides together, long edges even and using a 1 cm seam allowance, stitch 1 navy, 1 bright blue, 1 rust, then 1 red calico strip, along each long edge (hem edge) of rectangle. Trim seam allowances to 6 mm. Zigzag. On wrong side, press seam allowances toward rectangle. From right side, edgestitch each strip through all layers. Fold patched rectangle in half so hem edges meet. Cut out dress, being sure to place shoulders on fold. Slash back opening to dot as indicated.
Make tucks as follows: With wrong sides together, fold and press along solid lines indicated — first centre front fold, then folds on either side of centre front, then folds on either side of back opening, then one long fold running over each shoulder from front to back. Stitch tucks together along dotted lines. Press tucks toward sides. Narrowly hem back opening and sleeve edges. With right sides together, stitch side seams. Clip curves. Turn right side out. Turn under 1 cm, then 1 cm again around hem. Edgestitch along inside fold. Turn under 6 mm around neck edge, clipping curves if necessary. Pin gathered lace to inside neck edge so 1 cm shows above neck. From right side, topstitch lace in place. Overlap back opening edges to tucks and sew 2 snap fasteners in place.

7. **Nightgown:** Cut out nightgown from muslin, adding extra length as indicated. Make tucks as for dress. Narrowly hem back opening, neck edge and sleeve edges, clipping curves if necessary. Topstitch flat lace to right side of neck and sleeve edges. With right sides together, stitch side seams. Clip curves. Turn right side out. Hem. Attach snap fasteners as for dress.

8. Tie red ribbon in a bow around doll's neck. Trim ends.

4. **Pantaloons:** From pantaloon calico, cut 2 pantaloon pieces. With right sides together, stitch side seams. Turn under 6 mm (1/4 in) along hem edges. Pin flat lace to inside of hem edges so 1 cm (3/8 in) shows below hem. From right side, topstitch lace in place. With right sides together, stitch crotch seam. Clip curves. Turn right side out. To make casing for elastic, turn under 6 mm, then 10 mm (3/8 in) again around top edge. Edgestitch along inside fold, leaving a 1 cm opening at one side seam. Cut an 18 cm (7-in) length of elastic and thread through casing. Overlap ends 6 mm and join with hand stitches.

HEAVENLY CHOIR

Bring the spirit of Christmas into your home with a chorus of angelic choir girls (featured on the cover). Each caroler is simple to construct using a cardboard cone, a Styrofoam ball and bits of fabric — no sewing required.

DESIGN BY CAROL MOORE

Small choir girl stands 17 cm (6-3/4 in) tall, Medium stands 20 cm (7-7/8 in) tall and Large 24 cm (9-1/2 in) tall.

YOU NEED:
Quantities are given for Small size choir girl. Any changes for Medium and Large sizes are written in brackets. If there is only one set of figures, it applies to all three sizes.

- **Styrofoam ball, 4 (5,5) cm in diameter**
- **10 cm square of Dip and Drape fabric** *or* **cotton muslin and Fabri-Shape stiffener available at craft supply stores**
- **White 8-ply poster board, 21 × 16 (24 × 17, 32 × 24) cm, for body**
- **White sheer drapery fabric as follows: 23 × 17 (27.5 × 19.5, 31 × 26) cm, for dress**

- 18 × 7.5 (25 × 9, 27.5 × 10) cm, for sleeves
- **17 (20,23) cm of 24-gauge wire, for arms**
- **Kurly Kate rustless pot scrubber, for hair**
- **Straight pin**
- **White facial tissue**
- **Wooden skewer or knitting needle**
- **.50 m satin ribbon, 5 mm wide**

Who can resist creating an entire chorus of these no-sew choir girls? Arrange them as pictured here to decorate a table or mantel.

- **Birthday candle or white paper**
- **Gesso (white undercoat and sealer)**
- **Black, red and flesh-tone acrylic paint**
- **Artist's paintbrush**
- **Glue gun and glue sticks or white craft glue**
- **Elastic bands**
- **Brown paper**

CHOIR GIRL

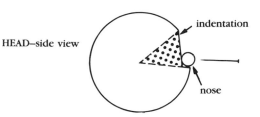

HEAD—side view

TO MAKE:

To enlarge pattern, see General Directions (page 134).

1. Roll half of Styrofoam ball along a sharp counter or table edge, making an indentation from one side of ball to other, for face (see Diagram for side view). Cut out a 10 mm (3/8-in) piece of Styrofoam from back of head, for nose. Press it between fingers to make a small ball about the size of a pea. With straight pin, attach nose to centre of face along indentation line. Place Dip and Drape fabric into very warm water for 5 seconds then shake off excess water or soak muslin in Fabri-Shape. Centre square over nose and mold it with fingers to fit around nose, cheeks, hairline and chin area. Set aside to dry in a warm place for about 4 hours. When face is dry and hard, paint with two coats of gesso allowing to dry at least 3 hours after each coat. Paint face with flesh-colored paint. Let dry. With point of skewer or knitting needle, poke a hole just below the nose and with a circular motion make an oval or circular hole for mouth. Paint eyes and inside of mouth with black paint. Put a tiny drop of red paint on your finger and gently rub into cheeks.

2. **Body:** Trace body pattern onto poster board. Cut out. Roll up sides to form a cone. Glue and hold together until dry. Apply glue to top of cone and push partway into head.

3. **Dress:** Fold dress fabric in half so short edges meet and right sides are together. Glue short edges together. Carefully turn right side out and slip tube over figure so seam is at back. Apply glue around neck. Pleat and gather fabric around neck, making a 2 to 2.5 cm (3/4- to 1-in) ruffle under chin. Hold gathers in place with elastic band until glue dries. Tuck and glue fabric at bottom of dress to inside of cone. Tie a small bow in middle

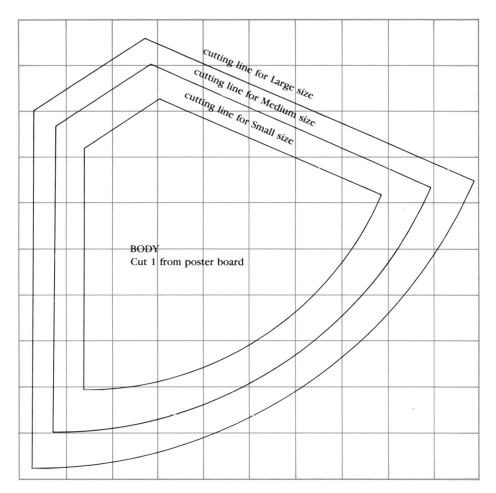

cutting line for Large size

cutting line for Medium size

cutting line for Small size

BODY
Cut 1 from poster board

of a 35 cm (13-3/4 in) length of ribbon and glue to front of dress just under ruffle at chin.

4. **Arms:** Fold sleeve fabric in half so long edges meet and wrong sides are together. Glue long edges together. Twist and glue a piece of tissue around wire so it is completely covered. Poke wire through sleeve tube. Apply glue to edges of fabric at each end of tube and to ends of wire. Pinch and gather fabric around ends of wire, holding in place with small elastic bands until glue dries. Centre arms across back of figure just below neck, hiding sleeve seam under arm. Glue in place. When glue is dry,

bend arms around to front of figure. Trim away any threads or frayed edges of fabric.

5. **Hair:** Run a line of glue around hairline on head. Fit pot scrubber over head (pull it apart into a smaller piece if too large) and hold in place with elastic bands until glue dries. Gently pull out curls. Tie remaining length of ribbon into a small bow and glue to top of head.

6. **Music book:** Cut a small rectangle of white paper and fold in half in shape of a book. Draw staff lines and musical notes. Glue to hands. If desired, glue a birthday candle to hands instead.

A TOY SOLDIER STORY

Adopt a "toy soldier" motif as your holiday theme and make your Christmas decorating extra special. The merry little soldier band is easy to make and makes a wonderfully whimsical display on a mantel or tabletop. Diminutive clothespeg soldiers can decorate a tree or hang from boughs arranged in a large drum for a table centrepiece. Miniature drums are perfect surprise containers for candy and nuts, and match the little napkin rings. Tuck crepe paper soldier hats inside your own Christmas crackers and you have a complete holiday table setting.

DESIGNS BY MARY CORCORAN

A happy Toy Soldier stands at attention next to his Graham Wafer Sentry Box (instructions, p. 29) while the band plays on.

TOY SOLDIER

YOU NEED:
- **Red felt as follows:**
  - 20.5 × 8 cm (8 × 3-1/8 in), for jacket
  - 2 pieces, each 9 × 2.5 cm (3-1/2 × 1 in), for sleeves
  - 2 circles, each 1 cm (3/8 in) in diameter, for cheeks
- **Black felt as follows:**
  - 23 × 14 cm (9 × 5-1/2 in), for legs
  - 7.5 cm (3 in) square, for feet
  - 20.5 cm × 6 mm (8 × 1/4 in), for belt
- **Piece of pink felt, 6.5 × 2 cm (2-1/2 × 3/4 in), for hands**
- **Piece of black fake fur, 18.5 × 10 cm (7-1/4 × 4 in), for hat**
- **Piece of pink cotton broadcloth,** 18 × 10 cm (7 × 4 in), for head
- **Matching threads**
- **.30 m gold ribbon, 3 mm wide**
- **.20 m gold braid, 10 mm wide**
- **2 tiny black beads**
- **6 tiny gold beads**
- **Polyester fibrefill**
- **Scotchgard**
- **Red felt-tip permanent marker**
- **Piece of black Bristol board, 7.5 cm square**

TOY SOLDIER

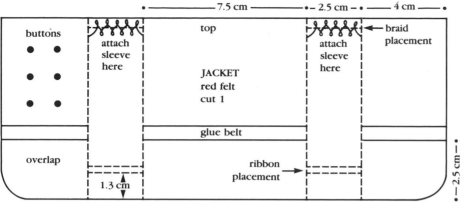

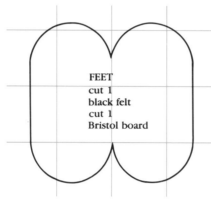

FEET
cut 1
black felt
cut 1
Bristol board

• **White craft glue**
• **Dressmaker's chalk pencil**
• **Brown paper**

TO MAKE:
To enlarge feet pattern, see General Directions (page 134).

1. **Head:** Following manufacturer's directions, spray pink broadcloth with Scotchgard. This will prevent facial features from running. Fold in half so right sides are together and short ends meet. Using a 6 mm (1/4-in) seam allowance, stitch seam opposite fold. Run a line of gathering stitches around both raw edges. Gather one end tightly. Knot threads. Turn right side out. Stuff head firmly with small amounts of fibrefill to within 13 mm (1/2 in) of open end. Gather, leaving a small opening. Knot threads. Stuff small pieces of fibrefill through hole into head to smooth out any wrinkles. Seam should be at side of head. Referring to photo, draw face on lower half of head with red marker. Using black thread, sew on black beads for eyes. Glue on red felt cheeks.

2. **Legs:** Fold leg piece in half so short ends meet. Stitch seam opposite fold. Turn right side out. Seam becomes centre front. Pin this seam to centre back line. Stitch down centre. Stuff legs lightly. Cut two 9 cm (3-1/2-in) lengths of gold ribbon. Glue these up side of each leg.

3. Place head on top of legs and slipstitch in place.

4. **Jacket:** Round off bottom corners of jacket piece as shown in Diagram. With

top edges even, glue or sew one end of each sleeve to top edge of jacket as shown in Diagram. Cut 2 lengths of gold braid and 2 lengths of ribbon, each 2.5 cm long. Glue braid across top of sleeves and ribbon across bottom of sleeves where indicated. With red thread, sew on 6 gold beads for buttons. Wrap jacket around upper half of soldier's body and overlap at front. Glue. Pin in place until glue dries. Glue belt around waist. Cut small piece of braid for buckle and glue to centre front of belt.

5. **Hands:** Fold pink felt in half so short ends meet. Cut along fold and round off corners at one end of each hand. Glue one hand under bottom edge of each sleeve, allowing 13 mm of hand to show below sleeves.

6. **Hat:** Fold piece of fake fur in half so right sides are together and short edges meet. Stitch up this seam and along one end. Turn right side out. Fit hat on soldier's head, positioning seam at side of head. For strap, wrap remaining length of braid under chin and tuck ends under hat on either side of head. Trim and glue ends in place.

7. **Feet:** Glue black felt square to Bristol board. Cut out feet. Check soldier's balance. Poke more stuffing into legs if necessary. Glue bottom of legs to centre of feet.

LITTLE DRUMMER

YOU NEED:
• **Piece of factory cotton (unbleached muslin), 14 × 11 cm (5-1/2 × 4-3/8 in)**
• **Red felt as follows:**
     12.5 × 3.2 cm (5 × 1-1/4 in), for jacket
     2 pieces, each 3.8 × 1.5 cm (1-1/2 × 5/8 in), for sleeves
• **Black felt as follows:**
     12 × 4.5 cm (4-3/4 × 1-3/4 in), for pants
     6 × 3.8 cm (2-3/8 × 1-1/2 in), for feet
• **Pink felt as follows:**
     3.2 × 1.5 cm (1-1/4 × 5/8 in), for hands
     circle, 2.2 cm (7/8 in) in diameter, for face
• **Piece of black fake fur, 9 × 6.5 cm (3-1/2 × 2-1/2 in), for hat**
• **Matching threads**
• **Gold thread**
• **.20 m gold ribbon, 3 mm wide**
• **5 cm gold braid, 10 mm wide**
• **Red and black embroidery floss**
• **2 red beads, 5mm in diameter**
• **6 tiny gold beads**
• **Polyester fibrefill**
• **2 round toothpicks**
• **Red pencil**
• **White craft glue**
• **Dressmaker's chalk pencil**
• **Brown paper**

TO MAKE:
For full-size pattern pieces, see page 135.

1. **Body:** Fold cotton in half so right sides are together and short edges meet. Trace around body pattern onto doubled fabric. Stitch along drawn line, leaving open at bottom where indicated. Cut out body, leaving a 6 mm (1/4-in) seam allowance around all edges. Clip curves. Turn right side out. Stuff firmly. Slipstitch opening closed.

2. **Face:** Using running stitch, sew pink

felt face to body, 6 mm below seam at top of head. Using 3 strands of black floss, embroider French knots for eyes. Embroider red mouth in stem stitch. Color cheeks with red pencil.

3. **Pants:** Wrap pants around lower half of body and overlap at centre front. Slipstitch in place. Cut two 3.8 cm lengths of gold ribbon. Glue these up side of each leg.

4. **Jacket:** Wrap jacket around upper half of body just below face and overlap at centre front. Slipstitch in place. Glue or sew one end of each sleeve to top edge on either side of jacket. Cut 2 lengths of gold braid and 2 lengths of ribbon, each 1.5 cm long. Glue braid across top of sleeves and ribbon across bottom of sleeves, 3 mm (1/8 in) from edge. With gold thread, sew 3 gold beads for buttons down jacket front, 6 mm to left of centre and another 3 to right of centre. Thread a loop of gold thread between 2 top buttons. Do the same between the two

Peg Soldier Ornament.

other pairs of parallel buttons. Cut a 1 cm (3/8-in) piece of braid and glue to centre front for belt buckle.

5. **Hands:** Fold pink felt in half so short ends meet. Cut along fold and round off corners at one end of each hand. Glue one hand under bottom edge of each sleeve, allowing 6 mm of hand to show below sleeves.

6. **Hat:** Fold piece of fake fur in half so right sides are together and short edges meet. Stitch up this seam and along one end. Turn right side out. Fit hat on drummer's head, positioning seam at side of head. For strap, wrap a length of ribbon under chin and tuck ends under hat on either side of head. Trim and glue ends in place.

7. **Drumsticks:** Cut off points at end of toothpicks. Glue red bead to one end of each toothpick and glue other end under each hand.

8. **Feet:** Cut feet from black felt. Glue to base of drummer.

PEG SOLDIER ORNAMENT

YOU NEED:
- **Piece of red felt, 5 cm × 6 mm (2 × 1/4 in)**
- **Scrap of black felt**
- **2 cm gold braid, 10 mm wide**
- **3.20 cm gold cord, 2 mm wide**
- **Gold thread**
- **5 m medium-weight black yarn**
- **Springless wooden clothespeg**
- **3 tiny gold beads**
- **Red, black and white acrylic paint**
- **Fine and medium artist's paintbrushes**
- **Black and red felt-tip permanent markers**
- **Piece of cardboard, 6.5 × 2 cm (2-1/2 × 3/4 in)**
- **White craft glue**

TO MAKE:

1. Paint knob on top of peg white, for head. Paint bottom 5.5 cm (2-1/8 in) black, for pants and middle section red, for jacket. Let dry. Mix red and white paint to make pink. Referring to Diagram, paint

pink cheeks and draw eyes and mouth with markers.

2. Cut red felt in half so you have 2 arms, 2.5 cm (1 in) long. Cut two 6 mm squares of black felt for hands. Round off corner on one end of each hand. Glue opposite end of hands to bottom of each arm. Glue arms to either side of peg, 6 mm down from neck.

3. Cut gold braid in half and glue one piece across each shoulder. Glue 3 beads down front of jacket, 6 mm apart. Glue gold cord under chin and up either side of face.

4. **Hat:** Thread darning needle with 30 cm (11-7/8-in) length of yarn. Fold so doubled. Wrap remaining yarn around width of cardboard. Slip needle under wrapped yarn on one side of cardboard. Gather up and tie as tightly as possible. Slide yarn off cardboard. Cut loops. Trim pom-pom into oval shape of bearskin hat. Glue on top of head.

5. Thread a hanging loop of gold thread through top of hat.

GRAHAM WAFER SENTRY BOX

YOU NEED:
- **2 egg whites**
- **5 mL (1 tsp) lemon juice**
- **750 mL/3 cups (approx) icing sugar**
- **Christie's graham wafers (the kind that are almost square — one 500 g package makes 2 sentry boxes)**
- **Granulated sugar**
- **Assorted candies such as jelly beans, cinnamon hearts and candy canes**
- **Baking sheet**
- **Large skillet (electric works best)**
- **Serrated-edged knife**
- **Piping bag and plain tip or a cone made from parchment or heavy waxed paper**
- **Wooden spoon**

TO MAKE ROYAL ICING:
Beat egg whites with lemon juice until stiff peaks form. Gradually beat in icing sugar until mixture is of spreading

consistency, or until knife drawn through leaves a clean sharp line.

Fill bag or cone three-quarters full, pushing icing into tip. Close wide end, folding sides toward middle and rolling top down to level of icing. Cover extra icing with a damp cloth to keep it from drying out. Keep at room temperature while building sentry box.

TO ASSEMBLE:

1. **Edible glue:** Put a 13 mm (1/2-in) layer of sugar in skillet. Heat, stirring with wooden spoon, over medium-high heat, until sugar melts. Reduce heat to keep melted sugar liquid (not tacky). This makes a quick-hardening edible glue, but is extremely hot. Caution: Do not touch or taste!

2. Arrange wafers (bumpy side down) on baking sheet in groups as shown in Diagram 1. Long side of wafer is width of sentry box, short side is the height. Rub all adjoining wafers together. This "sanding" gives edges a smoother finish for joining.

3. Glue each grouping together as follows: Dip one edge of wafer into hot syrup and glue it firmly to its neighbour on baking sheet. Keep dipped side of wafer down when lifting it from skillet, so glue doesn't touch skin. For large groupings, attach pairs of wafers together, then join pairs to each other.

4. Working on baking sheet, join sides to back so you have a three-sided building.

5. With serrated-edged knife, gently saw roof in half. Dip one short edge of each roof piece into syrup. Glue these to top edge of sides of sentry box, leaning pieces in toward centre to form peaked roof. Any gap along peak of roof will be hidden later with icing.

6. Gently saw peak from point A to points B on both sides (see Diagram 2). Large triangle is back peak. Discard one small triangle. Remaining small triangle is front peak. Glue front and back peaks in place along outer edges of roof. Gaps will be hidden later with icing.

TO DECORATE:

If using paper cone, cut off tip so icing will flow freely. Hold cone in left hand and wrap fingers of right hand around folds of cone (opposite for lefties). Direct

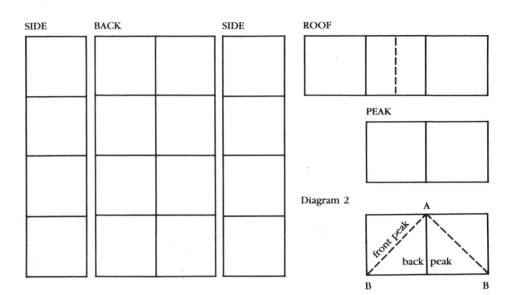

GRAHAM WAFER SENTRY BOX

Diagram 1

SIDE   BACK   SIDE   ROOF

PEAK

Diagram 2

front peak   back | peak

A

B   B

Graham Wafer Sentry Box.

cone to area to be iced, then squeeze. Keep icing in tip, near wafer. Using a zigzag pattern, ice over every seam. Decorate as desired, using icing and candies.

Let icing harden for about 24 hours in a dry place. Remove sentry box from cookie sheet and display in a dry place. If you want to preserve it for next Christmas, carefully pack it in a plastic bag and freeze, or spray it with several coats of urethane, wrap well in plastic and store in a dry place.

DRUM BONBON DISH

YOU NEED:
- **Piece of black felt, 20.5 × 9.5 cm (8 × 3-3/4 in)**
- **Piece of red felt, 20.5 × 2.5 cm (8 × 1 in)**
- **Black Bristol board, cut into the following pieces:**
    19.5 × 4.5 cm (7-5/8 × 1-3/4 in), for side of drum
    two 7.5 cm (3-in) squares, for lid and bottom
- **Piece of shiny gold paper, 15 × 7.5 cm (6 × 3 in)**
- **.90 m gold cord, 2 mm wide**
- **8 gold paper fasteners, size No. 3**

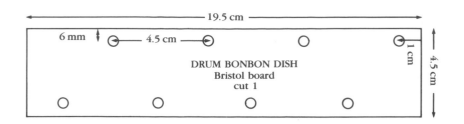

(available at office supply stores)
- **2 red wooden beads, 13 mm in diameter**
- **2 pieces of 1/8-in dowelling, each 7.5 cm (3 in) long**
- **Red and black thread**
- **White pencil**
- **Hole punch**
- **White craft glue**
- **Geometry compass**

TO MAKE:

1. Using white pencil and referring to Diagram, draw placement of holes on Bristol board side piece. Punch holes. Run board over sharp table edge so it curves to form a circle. Dab glue on outer surface. Centre and glue to black felt, allowing 2.5 cm felt overlap on long edges and 6 mm (1/4-in) overlap at ends.

2. Poke tip of scissors blade through punched holes into felt. Insert paper fasteners from felt side and open ends on wrong side to secure. Glue strip of red felt down centre of black felt between fasteners. Fold felt overlaps to inside, covering backs of fasteners. Glue in place.

3. Leaving a 23 cm (9-in) length of gold cord free at beginning, wrap cord around fastener at one end of drum. Carry it diagonally across to next fastener on opposite side and so on in zigzag fashion around all fasteners. Do not cut off extra cord.

4. Curve side piece up to form a tube and slipstitch ends together. Wrap extra cord around first fastener to complete zigzag formation.

5. Using compass and white pencil, draw two 6 cm (2-3/8-in) diameter circles on squares of black Bristol board. Cut out. From gold paper, cut 2 circles, each 3 mm (1/8 in) larger than Bristol board circles. Glue these to both sides of one Bristol board circle (lid). Punch hole close to edge of lid. Thread loose cord through hole and knot loosely to hold lid in place. Fit remaining circle into bottom of drum, trimming to fit if necessary.

6. To make drumsticks, glue a bead to one end of each dowel. Let dry. Slip drumsticks through knot on lid. Tighten knot and tie cord in a bow.

DRUM NAPKIN RING

YOU NEED:
- **Piece of black felt, 14 × 8 cm (5-1/2 × 3-1/8 in)**
- **Piece of red felt, 14 × 2 cm (5-1/2 × 3/4 in)**
- **Piece of Bristol board, 13.5 × 3.8 cm (5-3/8 × 1-1/2 in)**
- **.40 m gold cord, 2 mm wide**
- **Red and black thread**
- **6 gold paper fasteners, size No. 3 (available at office supply stores)**

- **White pencil**
- **Hole punch**
- **White craft glue**

TO MAKE:

1. Referring to Napkin Ring Diagram, follow Step 1 of Drum Bonbon Dish (this page), allowing a 2.2 cm (7/8-in) felt overlap on long edges.

2. Complete as for Drum Bonbon Dish (this page), Steps 2 to 4 but leave a 5 cm (2-in) end of cord at beginning of zigzag pattern. Glue ends of cord around fastener and trim.

DRUM CENTREPIECE

YOU NEED:
- **Clay flowerpot and saucer, 11.5 cm (4-1/2 in) in diameter**
- **Piece of black felt, 47 × 29 cm (18-1/2 × 11-1/2 in)**
- **Piece of red felt, 47 × 10 cm (18-1/2 × 4 in)**
- **Piece of black Bristol board, 56 × 28 cm (22 × 11 in)**
- **1.10 m gold cord, 3 mm wide**
- **1 m gold ribbon, 13 mm wide**
- **6 gold buttons, 15 mm in diameter**
- **Black thread**
- **Darning needle**
- **White craft glue**
- **Paper clips**
- **Gravel or stones to fill pot**
- **Pine or cedar branches**

TO MAKE:

1. Cut Bristol board in half lengthwise. Set one strip aside. On other strip, measure and mark a line 12.5 cm (5 in) from one end. This is the overlap. Run board over sharp table edge so it curves to form a circle. Overlap ends forming a tube. Glue, holding in place with paper clips until dry.

2. Spread glue around outer rims of drum. Centre and wrap black felt around drum, overlapping at seam. Glue overlap. Dab glue along long edges of red felt strip and wrap around centre of black felt. Glue overlap.

3. Mark positions for 3 buttons evenly

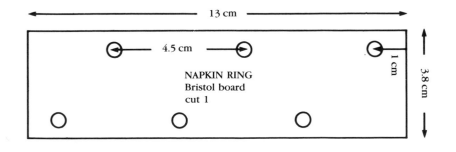

*This table setting would pass even a general's inspection. Centre back: Drum Centrepiece is filled
with cedar branches decorated with Peg Soldiers. Place setting: (left to right) Drum Bonbon Dish (p. 29),
Christmas Cracker (p. 32), Drum Napkin Ring (p. 30) and Little Drummer (p. 27).*

Snappy Christmas Crackers can be filled with surprises like the jaunty paper hat you can make yourself.

spaced (approx 14.5 cm/5-3/4 in apart) around bottom of drum, 13 mm (1/2 in) from rim of Bristol board, placing first button close to seam. Sew buttons in place through Bristol board and felt. Sew 3 buttons around top rim in same manner, spacing them midway between the bottom ones.

4. To reinforce drum, glue second strip of Bristol board inside drum. Glue felt overlaps to inside at top and bottom.

5. Cut ribbon in half. Glue each piece around drum along edges of red felt strip, overlapping ends at seam.

6. Starting at seam, thread cord around buttons as for Drum Bonbon Dish, page 30. Knot ends together. Trim.

7. Fill flowerpot with gravel and arrange branches in it. Place pot inside drum.

CHRISTMAS CRACKERS

YOU NEED: *(for each cracker)*
- **2 sheets of tissue paper in contrasting colors**
- **Red crepe paper (1 package makes approx 9 crackers)**
- **Piece of gold foil paper, 18 × 9 cm (7 × 3-1/2 in)**
- **Piece of black crepe paper, 18 × 6.5 cm (7 × 2-1/2 in)**

HAT FOR CHRISTMAS CRACKER

- **2 gold notary seals (available at office supply stores)**
- **.70 m gold cord, 2 mm wide**
- **Toilet paper roll**
- **1 snapper, 28 cm long**
- **Small favor to fit inside roll**
- **One-line saying, joke or fortune**
- **White craft glue**

TO MAKE HAT:

1. Fold one sheet of tissue paper in half lengthwise. Run finger along crease. Open out and lay flat. Fold in half widthwise. Fold corners at each end of fold down to centre line, forming peak.

2. Fold one layer of tissue at bottom of hat up to meet bottom edge of peak (see Diagram). Fold up the same again. Repeat for brim on other side. To hold brim together, dab glue on inside of brim at front and back of hat.

3. **Cockade:** Cut a piece of contrasting colored tissue paper, 38 × 23 cm (15 × 9 in). Fold in half lengthwise. Fold in half widthwise repeatedly until piece measures approx 11.5 × 2.5 cm (4-1/2 × 1 in). Cut fringe along raw edge every 6 mm (1/4 in) to a depth of 10 cm (4 in). Do not unfold. Tuck base of cockade 13 mm (1/2 in) under brim on one side of hat. Glue notary seal over brim and cockade to hold in place.

4. Fold up hat so it will fit into toilet paper roll.

TO MAKE CRACKER:

1. Stuff toilet paper roll with snapper, hat, favor and joke.

2. Cut two 25.5 cm (10-in) squares of red crepe paper. Wrap both layers around roll (so roll runs along grain of paper). Glue in place. Fringe ends by cutting every 6 mm to a depth of 2.5 cm.

3. Cut gold cord in half. Tie one piece tightly around crepe paper and snapper at each end of roll. Tie in a bow.

4. Wrap strip of gold paper around centre of cracker. Glue in place. Centre and wrap strip of black crepe paper around cracker over gold paper. Glue in place. Glue notary seal in centre of cracker.

MERRY MOUSE CHOIR

'Twas the night before Christmas/Church bells had stopped ringing/
Most folks were asleep/But the mice were still singing . . .

*Stitched from bits of felt, broadcloth and eyelet, and complete with little
songbooks, this delightful mouse chorus looks great on a mantel or on a
cheese box as a table decoration.*

DESIGN BY CAROLYN SMITH

YOU NEED: *(for each mouse)*
- **Piece of grey felt, 23 × 15 cm (9 × 6 in)**
- **Scrap of red felt, 5 × 2.5 cm (2 × 1 in)**
- **Piece of red broadcloth, 16 × 11.5 cm (6-1/4 × 4-1/2 in)**
- **.20 m flat eyelet lace, 75 mm wide**
- **Matching threads**
- **Grey buttonhole twist thread, for whiskers**
- **2 black beads, for eyes**
- **Polyester fibrefill**
- **Piece of white paper, 5 × 2.5 cm**
- **Black fine-tip permanent marker**
- **White craft glue**
- **Brown paper**

TO MAKE:

For full-size pattern pieces, see page 135.

1. Cut all pieces from grey felt.

2. Using a short running stitch, sew head/body pieces together close to outer edge, leaving open at bottom. Stitching will show on right side. Make a 6 mm (1/4-in) slit for ears on each side of head as indicated. Roll ear piece lengthwise and push through one ear slit and out the other. Stuff head/body with small amounts of fibrefill, adjusting ears if necessary. Stitch base to bottom of body.

3. Sew on bead eyes. Thread a needle with grey thread for whiskers. Push needle through snout from one side to the other. Cut thread leaving a 2 cm (3/4-in) whisker on each side of snout. Thread through 2 more sets of whiskers in same manner. Stiffen whiskers with clear nail polish if desired.

4. **Choir gown:** Turn under 6 mm on one long edge and both short edges of red fabric. Hem. Turn under approx 13 mm (1/2 in) on remaining raw edge (neck edge). Check length on mouse and adjust if necessary. Run a line of gathering stitches around neck, 1 cm (3/8 in) from folded edge. Pull up thread to fit around mouse's neck. Knot ends. Fit gown on mouse, positioning opening at back. Slipstitch top half of back opening closed.

5. **Surplice:** Locate centre point along length of eyelet lace. Measure and mark points 2.5 cm to either side of centre and 5 cm up from finished edge. Make a 6 mm slit at these 2 points. Slip straight end of paw through each slit and slipstitch in place on wrong side of eyelet. Turn under 6 mm then 6 mm again on both ends of eyelet. Hem. Turn under 6 mm along remaining raw edge (neck edge) of eyelet. Run a line of gathering stitches around neck close to fold. Fit surplice on mouse, positioning opening at back. Adjust gathers to fit around neck. Knot ends. Slipstitch edges together at neck.

6. **Hymn book:** With black marker, draw musical notes on one side of piece of paper. Glue to scrap of red felt and bend in half to form book. Glue book between paws.

7. Stitch straight end of tail to base at centre back. Stitch remaining paws to base on either side of centre front.

Canadian Living

GLORIOUS CHRISTMAS CRAFTS

TREE TRIMS

CHAPTER II

NUTCRACKER ORNAMENTS

Set a magical mood with tree trims inspired by The Nutcracker.
*Tiny felt ornaments such as Toy Soldier, Drum, Mouse and Ballet
Slippers will bring the wonder of this famous ballet into your
home during the Christmas season.*

DESIGNS BY RENÉE SCHWARZ

FELT TOY SOLDIER ORNAMENT

Finished ornament is 16 cm (6-1/4 in) tall.

YOU NEED:

- **Piece of flesh-tone cotton or unbleached muslin, 10 × 6 cm (4 × 2-3/8 in)**
- **Scrap of black felt, 13 × 12 cm (5-1/8 × 4-3/4 in), for hat and boots**
- **Scrap of royal blue felt, 10 × 6 cm, for pants**
- **Scrap of red felt, 12 × 7 cm (4-3/4 × 2-3/4 in), for shirt**
- **Scrap of white felt, 8 × 5 cm (3-1/8 × 2 in), for hands, cross and brush**
- **16 cm gold braid, 3 mm wide**
- **14 cm flat gold braid, 9 mm wide**
- **Matching threads**
- **Invisible nylon thread**
- **Small amount polyester fibrefill**
- **Navy, black, brown and red acrylic or fabric paint *or* embroidery floss**
- **White craft glue**
- **Brown paper**

TO MAKE:

For full-size pattern pieces, see page 137.

1. **Head:** From flesh-tone cotton, cut 2 heads. With right sides together and using a 6 mm (1/4-in) seam allowance, sew heads together, leaving open at top. Turn right side out. Stuff. Slipstitch opening closed. Paint or embroider navy eyes, red cheeks, brown nose and chin and black moustache.

2. **Body:** From red felt, cut 2 shirts. From blue felt, cut 2 pants. From black felt, cut 2 boots. From white felt, cut 2 hands and 1 cross. Overlap top edge of boot 6 mm over bottom edge of pants. Edgestitch in place. Repeat with other boot and pants pieces. Place boots/pants pieces wrong sides together and edgestitch boots together around outside edge. Topstitch down centre of boots. Stuff.
Overlap bottom edge of shirt 6 mm over top edge of pants. Edgestitch in place. Repeat with other shirt piece on other side of pants. Edgestitch pants together down outside edges. Topstitch up centre of pants from boots to 1 cm (3/8 in) from shirt.
Place hands between shirt sleeves so they project 1 cm beyond cuff. Edgestitch shirt together around outside edges, leaving open at neck. Stuff body. Insert neck into shirt neck opening. Edgestitch in place by hand. Glue cross onto front of shirt.

3. **Hat:** From black felt, cut 2 hats and from white felt, cut 1 brush. With right sides together and using a 6 mm seam allowance, sew hat pieces together, leaving bottom edge open. Turn right side out. Stuff lightly. Turn under 3 mm (1/8 in) around bottom edge. Pin to head. Sew base of brush to centre front of hat. Tie a double knot in centre of narrow gold braid and hand-stitch this knot in place over base of brush. Bring ends of braid around to back of head and tuck under hat. Slipstitch hat in place, catching braid ends in stitching.

4. Sew 9 cm (3-1/2-in) length of wide gold braid around waist, overlapping and turning under ends at back. Cut two 2.5 cm (1-in) lengths of wide gold braid for epaulettes. Fold ends under and hand-stitch to each shoulder.

5. Thread hanging loop of invisible thread through top of hat.

FELT MOUSE ORNAMENT

Finished ornament is 10 cm (4 in) tall.

YOU NEED:

- **Piece of grey felt, 28 × 12 cm (11 × 4-3/4 in)**
- **Small scrap of black felt**
- **14 cm silver cord, 3 mm wide**
- **Matching thread**
- **Invisible nylon thread**
- **Black buttonhole twist thread**
- **Black embroidery floss**
- **Small amount polyester fibrefill**
- **10.5 cm thin wire, 1 mm thick**
- **No. 22 tapestry needle, for sword**
- **Brown paper**

TO MAKE:

For full-size pattern pieces, see page 137.

1. **Head:** From grey felt, cut 1 head and a rectangle approx 7 × 6 cm (2-3/4 × 2-3/8 in). Place cutout head on rectangle and edgestitch pieces together around outside edge of head, leaving

A Felt Toy Soldier Ornament to charm the young and young at heart.

Felt Mouse brandishes his playful sword. Instructions begin on p. 36.

FELT DRUM ORNAMENT

Finished ornament is 8 × 7.5 cm (3-1/8 × 3 in).

YOU NEED:
- **Piece of white felt, 18 × 9 cm (7 × 3-1/2 in)**
- **Piece of red felt, 10 × 9 cm (4 × 3-1/2 in)**
- **.70 m gold braid, 3 mm wide**
- **Matching threads**
- **Small amount polyester fibrefill**
- **Brown paper**

TO MAKE:
For full-size pattern pieces, see page 138.

1. From white felt, cut 2 drums and from red felt, cut 4 bands.

2. Position gold braid along zigzag broken lines on each drum piece, tacking in place at each corner. On each drum piece, position one band so lower edge extends 6 mm (1/4 in) below bottom edge of drum and another band the same way up at top edge of drum, having top corners matching. Edgestitch upper edge of bottom band and both long edges of top band in place on each drum.

3. Pin decorated drum pieces wrong sides together. Cut a 21 cm (8-1/4-in) length of braid. Sandwich ends between felt at top corners of drum, forming a handle. Changing thread color where appropriate, edgestitch drum pieces together around outside edges, leaving a small opening along one side. Stuff lightly. Edgestitch opening closed.

open between ears. Trim rectangle to shape of head. Stuff lightly. Edgestitch opening closed. Using 2 strands of floss and satin stitch, embroider eyes and nose. Thread 2 lengths of buttonhole thread through snout for whiskers. Trim.

2. **Body:** From grey felt, cut 1 body and a rectangle approx 11 × 9 cm (4-3/8 × 3-1/2 in). Edgestitch cutout body to rectangle (leaving opening at neck), trim felt, stuff and close opening as for head. Hand-stitch head to front of body at neck.

3. **Tail:** From grey felt, cut a strip 12 × 3 cm (4-3/4 × 1-1/8 in). Fold strip in half lengthwise over wire. Making sure that wire is enclosed in the fold, stitch long edges together 4 mm (3/16 in) from fold, ending stitching in a point 6 mm

(1/4 in) from one end. Trim felt to 3 mm (1/8 in) from seam. Bend tail into S shape and stitch open end to middle of mouse's back, approx 3 cm up from bottom of feet.
Fold silver cord in half to form a loop. Sew together 1 cm (3/8 in) from ends. Slip loop diagonally over mouse's shoulder.

4. **Sword:** Sew tapestry needle to palm of mouse's left hand, stitching through eye of needle. Fold hand over eye of needle and stitch in place. Cut a 1.3 cm (1/2-in) diameter circle from black felt. Slip circle onto sword and attach to top of hand with a dab of glue.

5. Thread hanging loop of invisible thread through top of head.

Felt Drum Ornament.

Felt Ballet Slippers Ornament.

FELT BALLET SLIPPERS ORNAMENT

Finished ornament is approx 12 × 11 cm (4-3/4 × 4-3/8 in).

YOU NEED (*for pair of slippers*):
- **Piece of white felt, 42 × 18 cm (16-1/2 × 7 in)**
- **1.60 m satin ribbon, 9 mm wide**
- **2 small gold bows**
- **Matching thread**
- **Small amount polyester fibrefill**
- **Brown paper**

TO MAKE:

For full-size pattern, see page 137.

1. From felt, cut 3 slipper pieces. Cut inside oval-shaped section out of 2 (for shoe upper) of these 3 pieces.

2. Pin 2 shoe upper pieces together. Edgestitch, then satin-stitch around edge of centre cutout. Insert a small amount of fibrefill between the 2 layers. With right sides together, pin upper to remaining piece (slipper sole). Stitch together using a 6 mm (1/4-in) seam allowance. Turn right side out.

3. Cut two 40 cm (15-3/4-in) lengths of ribbon. Sew one end of each to inside side edges of slipper. Sew bow on top front of slipper.

4. Make a second slipper in same manner, following Steps 1 to 3. Knot and tie loose ends of ribbons from each slipper together in a bow. Stitch through knot to secure. To hold slippers together as a pair, tack sides together.

ANGELIC ORNAMENTS

*Each of these four heavenly ornaments has a personality of its own.
Angelica has a mop of orange hair, feathery wings and waves a magic
wand. Mini Angel is a miniature felt version of the heirloom Treetop Angel
(page 68). Angel Fluff may very well be the tiniest ornament on your
tree. And for anyone who likes to work with wood, Cheeky Little Angel is
a whimsical charmer. All are guaranteed to capture everyone's heart.*

Angelica, the mischievous little tree trim.

ANGELICA

Design by Joan Doherty

YOU NEED:
- **Piece of white cotton broadcloth,
  30 × 15 cm (11-7/8 × 6 in)**
- **Piece of pink felt, 8 cm (3-1/8 in)
  square**
- **Scrap of red felt**
- **Blue, black, brown, red and pink
  liquid embroidery**
- **Small amount of fleece, dyed orange
  or yellow (available at weaving
  stores)**
- **Matching threads**
- **Invisible nylon thread**
- **2 white feathers, approx 8 cm long**
- **Gold tinsel wire, 14 cm (5-1/2 in) long**
- **Gold glitter**
- **Gold paint**
- **Little bunch of tiny artificial flowers**
- **Polyester fibrefill**
- **Toothpick, for wand**
- **Piece of cardboard, 5 cm (2 in) square**
- **White craft glue**
- **Brown paper**

TO MAKE:
For full-size pattern pieces, see page 136.

1. Cut 2 angel bodies from broadcloth,
adding a 6 mm (1/4-in) seam allowance
on all edges. From pink felt, cut 1 face
and 2 hands. From red felt, cut 1 heart.

2. Using a narrow zigzag stitch, appliqué
face to right side of 1 body piece. With
liquid embroidery, draw blue eyes with
black pupils, brown eyebrows and
nostrils, red mouth and pink cheeks.

3. With right sides together, sew body
front to back around curved edge, using
a 6 mm seam allowance. Turn right side
out. Stuff firmly. Turn under 6 mm around
bottom edge and slipstitch closed.

4. Arrange fleece hair on angel's head.
Bend gold tinsel wire around hair to look
like a halo. Tack hair and halo in place
on each side of head. Stick flowers into
halo on one side of head.

5. From cardboard, cut 1 star. Glue end

of toothpick to star, for wand. Cover both sides of star with glue and dip in glitter. Let dry. Paint toothpick gold. Let dry. Sew wand to front of angel with a few tiny stitches. Glue hands over wand, hiding the stitches. Glue heart in place.

6. Poke feathers in back of angel. Thread a hanging loop of invisible thread through top of head.

MINI ANGEL

Design by Carol Schmidt

This is the miniature version of the Treetop Angel on page 68.

YOU NEED:
- **Piece of white felt, 16 × 12 cm (6-1/4 × 4-3/4 in)**
- **Scrap of flesh-tone felt**
- **Crocheted doily, approx 9 cm (3-1/2 in) in diameter**
- **10 cm white lace, 10 mm wide**
- **White thread**
- **Brown and red embroidery floss**
- **Gold embroidery thread such as DMC Fil Or**
- **No. 8 white DMC coton perlé**
- **Polyester fibrefill**
- **Small artist's paintbrush**
- **Powder blush**

TO MAKE:
For full-size pattern, see page 138.

1. From white felt, cut 2 angel bodies. From flesh-tone felt, cut face and hands.

2. Sew face and hands to front body using tiny backstitches. With one strand of floss and using small outline stitches, embroider brown eyes and red mouth. With white coton perlé, embroider 3 mm (1/8-in) long backstitches up centre front and around yoke area on each side of hands. Starting at bottom, lace gold thread in and out of backstitches up one side to face. Embroider French knots around face, for hair, wrapping thread twice around needle for each knot. Continue lacing thread down backstitches on opposite side. With gold thread, embroider one flower on each side of front, using detached chain or lazy daisy stitch for petals and French knot for centre.

3. With right sides together, sew front to back using a 6 mm (1/4-in) seam allowance and leaving open at bottom. Clip curves. Turn right side out. Stuff lightly. Turn under 6 mm around bottom edge. Baste lace along inside of bottom edge, turning raw ends toward back. Backstitch opening closed.

4. Fold doily in half and tack to back of angel for wings. Using paintbrush, highlight cheeks with a little blush.

5. Thread hanging loop of gold thread through top of angel.

ANGEL FLUFF

Design by Louise Chisholm

YOU NEED:
- **6 cm (2-3/8-in) circle of white cotton fabric**
- **12 cm white eyelet lace, 25 mm wide**
- **1.25 m gold thread**
- **White thread**
- **Small amounts of blue, gold and pink embroidery floss**
- **Small amount of polyester fibrefill**
- **2 small white feathers**
- **1 white plastic flower stamen**

A sweet-faced, delicately winged Mini Angel.

*She's just a little "fluff" of an angel.
Instructions begin on p. 41.*

TO MAKE:

1. Transfer face (shown actual size below) onto centre of fabric circle. Using 2 strands of floss, embroider blue eyes, gold eyebrows and pink nose and mouth.

ANGEL FLUFF

FACE
(actual size)

2. Run a line of gathering stitches around edge of circle. Place small amount of fibrefill on wrong side. Pull up gathering thread as tightly as possible and secure.

3. Fold stamen into a V for arms and stitch to back of head. Run a line of gathering stitches along straight edge of eyelet lace. Gather into a circle and stitch to back of head.

4. Set aside 15 cm (6 in) of gold thread for hanging loop. Wind remaining gold thread around 2 fingers. Tie loops in

centre and stitch to top of head for hair.

5. Poke feathers behind neck on each side of head for wings. Stitch in place. Make a tiny bow from pink floss. Stitch in place at front neck.

6. Thread hanging loop of gold thread through top of eyelet.

CHEEKY LITTLE ANGEL

Design by Jane Buckles

YOU NEED:

- **Scraps of pine, 1 × 6 × 6 in and 1/2 × 5/8 × 2-1/2 in**
- **3/8-in dowelling, 4 in long**
- **1/8-in dowelling, 4 in long**
- **12 cm coat hanger wire, for halo**
- **1.10 m orange craft yarn, for hair**
- **White craft glue**
- **Flesh, red and blue colored pencils**
- **Black fine-tip permanent marker**
- **White and gold paint**
- **Electric drill with 1/8-in and 3/16-in**

bits
- **Band or jigsaw**
- **Hand saw**
- **Sandpaper**
- **Pliers**
- **Screw eye**

TO MAKE:

1. Transfer angel outline (shown actual size on page 136) onto large piece of pine. Using band or jigsaw, cut out shape. Cut remaining scrap of pine into 2 pieces, each 1/2 × 5/8 × 1-1/4 in, for feet. Cut 3/8-in dowelling into 2 pieces, each 2 in long, for legs, and cut 1/8-in dowelling into 1 piece, 2-1/2 in long, for leg pin, and 2 pieces, 3/4 in long, for foot pins. Sand all pieces lightly.

2. Drill 1/8-holes for leg pin, horizontally straight through bottom of body as shown. Drill 3/16-in holes for leg pin horizontally through top of each leg, 3/16 in from end. Drill 1/8-in hole in bottom of each leg and in top of each foot as shown. Drill 15, 1/8-in holes in top of head to accommodate hair and halo.

3. Bend one end of wire into a 1-in diameter circle. Bend other end straight down to form stem of halo.

4. Color face with flesh colored pencil. Paint body and feet white. When dry, transfer wing and arm markings; then paint gold. Paint legs and halo gold. Draw facial features with black marker and color in eyes with blue pencil and cheeks and mouth with red.

5. Apply glue in horizontal holes at bottom of body. Insert leg pin from one side of body, through outer hole, through hole in one leg, through middle hole, through hole in other leg and out through outer hole. Legs should move freely. Glue foot pins into bottom of legs and into holes in feet.

6. Insert screw eye into top of head and glue stem of halo into one of the holes in centre top of head.

7. Cut yarn into 13 pieces. Fold each piece in half. Dab glue on fold and poke into remaining holes in head with a nail or darning needle. When glue is dry, trim hair. Attach hanging thread or ribbon to screw eye.

*Movable legs make Cheeky Little Angel a unique ornament.
Make several for a heavenly tree.*

Hanging from the tree boughs are: (clockwise from top) Bear, Girl,
Owl, Walrus, Boy, Bird and Sundial Face.

INUIT INSPIRATIONS

Sometimes the simplest ideas for tree trims fashion the best theme trees. The figurative drawings of the Inuit are the inspiration for a charming collection of baker's clay ornaments. Make all seven designs for a unique tree.

DESIGNS BY ANN BOUFFARD

YOU NEED:
- **For baker's clay (12 to 14 ornaments):**
  - 1 cup (250 mL) all-purpose flour
  - 1/2 cup (125 mL) salt
  - 1/2 cup (125 mL) water
- **Black peppercorns**
- **Toothpicks**
- **Paper clip**
- **Wire or hairpins**
- **Small pointed knife**
- **Foil**
- **Spatula**
- **Baking sheet**
- **Polyurethane varnish (optional)**

TO MAKE CLAY:

Mix together ingredients for clay to form a soft dough. Working on a floured board, knead until smooth, about 8 to 10 minutes. Clay is very workable and can be easily bent, pinched or molded into desired shapes. Shape each figure and flatten to between 6 mm (1/4-in) and 13 mm (1/2-in) thickness. To attach pieces, moisten each with a little water. With spatula, lift finished figures onto foil and place on baking sheet. Bake in 250°F (120°C) oven for 4 to 5 hours or until thoroughly dry. Finish with varnish if desired.

TO SHAPE FIGURES:

BIRD

1. **Body:** Roll a ball of clay 4 cm (1-1/2 in) in diameter. Roll this out into a 10 cm (4-in) teardrop shape with points at both ends. Pinch ends to finer points for tail and beak. Lift head up and push slightly toward back to give bird a chest. Press in peppercorn for eye.

2. **Wing:** Roll a ball of clay 2 cm (3/4 in) in diameter. Roll this out into a 7.5 cm (3-in) teardrop shape. Attach to body.

Curve wing and tail up slightly toward back. With knife, mark feathers on wing.

3. **Claws:** Roll 2 tiny balls into short lengths. Attach to underside of body and bend tips downward (see photo).

4. Make a small U-shaped loop from wire or hairpin. Moisten and insert into top of bird, slightly forward on body for balance.

OWL

1. **Body:** Roll a 4 cm ball into a 7.5 cm teardrop shape. Flatten with heel of hand to approx 13 mm thickness.

2. **Head:** Roll a 2 cm ball. Flatten and attach to wide end of body. Pinch front of head to form owl face (see photo). Press in peppercorns for eyes. Blend head into body by rubbing area with moistened finger.

3. **Wing:** Roll a 2 cm ball into a 6.5 cm (2-1/2-in) teardrop shape. Flatten and attach to body. With knife, mark feathers on wing and body.

4. **Claws:** Roll 2 pea-size balls into short lengths. Attach to underside of body and bend tips downward.

5. Moisten and insert wire loop into top of head.

WALRUS

1. **Body:** Roll a 4 cm ball into a 10 cm teardrop shape. Flatten slightly. Pinch at wide end for neck and at pointed end for base of tail. With knife, slit tail in half and mark indentations.

2. **Head:** Raise head and push slightly toward back (see photo). If head will not stay up, clay is too moist — add flour and try again. Poke holes for snout with toothpick. Press in peppercorns for eyes.

3. **Tusks:** Roll 2 very tiny teardrop shapes and attach to head on either side of snout.

4. **Fin:** Roll a pea-size ball into a teardrop shape. Attach to lower body; mark indentations with knife.

5. Moisten and insert wire loop into top of body.

BEAR

1. **Body:** Roll a 4 cm ball into a 10 cm teardrop shape. Flatten. Pinch pointed end slightly to a finer point for nose. Make cut for mouth.

2. **Legs:** Roll 2 pea-size balls into 13 mm lengths. Do not flatten. Attach to underside of body for bottom legs. Roll two 2.5 cm (1-in) balls into 5 cm (2-in) teardrop shapes for top legs. Flatten slightly and attach to body so they are supported by bottom legs. Bend tips of all legs forward to form paws.

3. **Head:** Press in peppercorns for eye and nose. Make a tiny teardrop shape for ear and attach to head.

4. Moisten and insert wire loop into top of body.

SUNDIAL FACE

Flatten a 5 cm ball. Roll seven 6 mm balls; flatten and attach these around face. Roll out a long, thin length and attach around sundial face inside circles. Attach tiny pieces of clay for mouth and nose. Mark eyes with knife.

GIRL

1. **Parka:** Roll a 4 cm ball into a 6.5 cm length, slightly smaller at one end. Flatten slightly.

2. **Head:** Roll a 13 mm ball, flatten

slightly and attach to top of parka (smaller end). Mark eyes with knife. Make a curved mouth by pressing in with small end of paper clip. Attach a tiny ball for nose and 2 slightly larger balls, flattened, for cheeks.

3. **Hood:** Roll a 2.5 cm ball into a 7.5 cm length; attach around head.

4. **Skirt:** Roll a 2 cm ball into a 5 cm length and attach to bottom of parka. Press with little finger to create ruffle effect.

5. **Boots:** Roll 2 balls the size of large peas into 2.5 cm lengths. Attach to bottom of skirt and bend tips up to form feet.

6. **Arms:** Roll two 2.5 cm balls into 6.5 cm lengths, each slightly smaller at one end. Flatten slightly. Attach larger ends to shoulders. Bend arms forward across parka.

7. **Hands:** Roll 2 pea-size balls, flatten and attach to arms. Make tiny slashes for thumbs.

8. **Trim:** Roll out lengths 3 to 6 mm (1/8 to 1/4 in) wide and attach at collar, cuffs and bottom of parka and at top of boots. Mark trim and hood with knife for fur texture effect. With end of paper clip, poke holes down front of boots (see photo). Press peppercorns for buttons.

9. Moisten and insert wire loop into top of head.

BOY

1. Make parka, head and hood as for girl.

2. **Legs:** Roll two 2 cm balls into 4 cm lengths, each slightly smaller at one end. Flatten slightly and attach larger ends to bottom of parka. Bend tips up to form feet.

3. **Arms:** Roll two 2 cm balls into 4 cm lengths, each slightly smaller at one end. Flatten slightly and attach larger ends to shoulders so arms are raised.

4. Make holes down boots, hands and trim as for girl, adding extra trim down front of parka instead of buttons. Mark trim and hood with knife for fur texture effect.

5. Moisten and insert wire loop into top of head.

KNITTED GINGERBREAD MAN

Knit a whole batch of gingerbread men. Then use them to decorate a tree or a special gift, or give them as lovable little toys. They'll look good enough to eat!

DESIGN BY JEAN SCOBIE

Knitting a gingerbread man is simple. Beginning at the feet, knit a rectangle, shaping at the top for the head. When the body is sewn together and stuffed, the arms and legs are defined by stitching through all layers. Embroidered details are added at the end.

YOU NEED:
- Small quantity of gingerbread-brown Sayelle or similar-weight yarn
- Scraps of dark brown, white and red yarn
- One pair 3.00 mm needles
- Tapestry needle
- Invisible nylon thread
- Polyester fibrefill

TO MAKE:
See General Directions (page 134) for knitting abbreviations.

Work in St st throughout.
Cast on 32 sts.
Work 20 rows for legs. Place marker at end of row.
Work 14 rows for upper body. Place marker at end of row to indicate neck.
Work 15 rows for head as follows:
Rows 1-8: Work even in St st.
Row 9: Dec 5 sts evenly across row (27 sts rem).
Row 10: Purl.
Row 11: Dec 5 sts evenly across row (22 sts rem).
Row 12: Purl.

A crate of Knitted Gingerbread Men ready for holiday decorating.

Row 13: Dec 5 sts evenly across row (17 sts rem).

Row 14: Purl.

Row 15: K1, (k2 tog) 8 times. Draw yarn through rem sts and pull up.

TO FINISH:

1. Sew sides tog to form centre back seam.

2. Stuff head. Weave a single strand of matching yarn through neck row. Draw up and tie tightly.

3. Stuff body and sew bottom opening closed, pulling in as much as possible.

4. With matching yarn, define arms by sewing small back stitches through all layers from waist to 2 rows below neck.

Define legs in same manner, from bottom edge to just below waistline.

5. Embroider arm outline, ankles, mouth, eyes and buttons with colored yarn.

6. Thread a hanging loop of invisible thread through top of head.

SAUCY SANTAS

Let children capture the magic of the season with their own little tree. Cone-shaped paper Santas are the perfect project for the kindergarten crowd — with a little help from you.

DESIGN BY SISTER
CATHERINE MARY STRONG

YOU NEED:
- **Red construction paper**
- **White typing paper**
- **Red felt-tip marker**
- **Red thread**
- **White craft glue**
- **Clothespin**
- **Needle**
- **Geometry compass**

TO MAKE:

1. Using compass, draw a 29 cm (11-1/2-in) diameter circle on red construction paper. Cut out. Cut circle into 4 equal pie-shaped wedges.

2. Using photo as a guide, cut a Santa face and beard from white paper. Draw eyes and mouth. Glue to centre of one wedge.

3. Roll up sides of wedge to form a cone, overlapping edges 13 mm (1/2 in). Glue in place. Hold together with clothespin until glue dries.

4. Thread a loop of red thread through tip of cone. Make Santas from 3 remaining wedges in the same manner.

A child's theme tree of Saucy Santas.

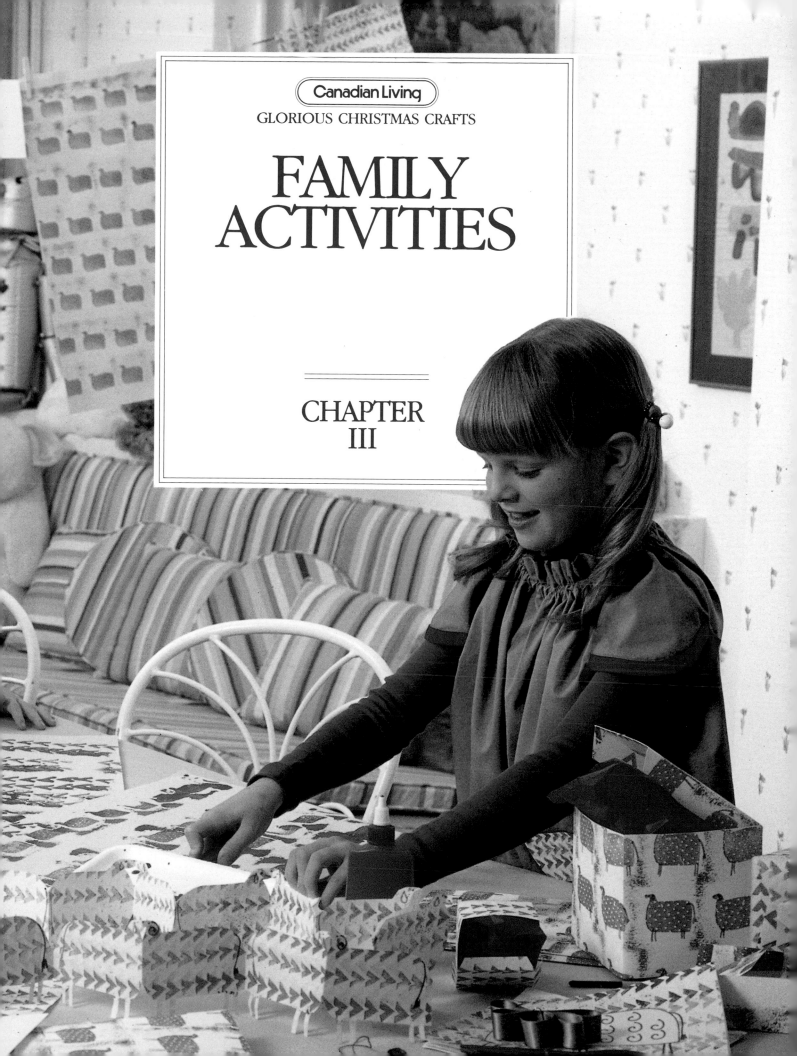

Canadian Living
GLORIOUS CHRISTMAS CRAFTS

FAMILY ACTIVITIES

CHAPTER III

FESTIVE ROLLER PRINTING

Children love to participate in holiday preparations. With easy-to-do roller printing projects they can create their own practical Christmas presents, cards, decorations and gift wrap. The stencils and rollers are designed to be used on paper and fabric. Make the cheerful Child's Play Smock to keep your little artist's clothes clean.

DESIGNS BY MARY CORCORAN

Printing with a plain roller is very easy and gives a mottled, textured effect. To make a patterned roller requires an adult's help.

PRINTING

YOU NEED:
- Small paint roller, approx 9 cm (3-1/2 in) wide
- Pair of shoe insoles (preferably men's size large) with foam rubber backing, with or without perforations, for making patterned roller
- Paper such as newsprint, shelf paper, construction paper, artist's drawing paper, Bristol board *or* factory cotton (unbleached muslin), depending on the individual project
- Poster paint (tempera) for paper printing
- Non-toxic, water-soluble fabric paint for fabric printing
- Paintbrush
- Non-toxic, washable felt-tip markers
- Contact cement
- Toothpick
- Masking tape
- Flat, smooth Styrofoam or foil tray
- Tracing paper
- Newspaper or plastic tablecoth

TO MAKE PATTERNED ROLLER:

1. Trace small sheep and small or large V motifs (below) onto tracing paper or design your own motifs. Cut out.

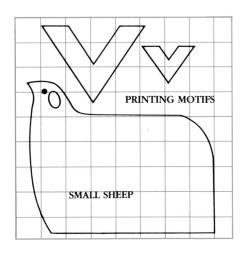

PRINTING MOTIFS

SMALL SHEEP

2. Trace around paper patterns onto fabric side of insole. You can use several small motifs on each roller. Cut out carefully.

3. Use toothpick to spread contact cement on fabric side of insole cutouts. Glue these evenly spaced around roller. Be sure to fill the width of the roller.

Plain or patterned rollers and a stencil are all you need to make a houseful of Christmas gifts, wrappings and decorations.

TO PRINT ON PAPER:

1. Cover work surface with newspaper or plastic tablecloth.

2. Following manufacturer's directions, mix poster paint with water until it is the consistency of milk. Brush a thin layer onto tray. Run roller through paint. When using patterned roller, make sure motifs are well coated with paint. For mottled, fleecy effect, use the plain roller almost dry. Roll onto desired paper. One long steady roll gives best results. Run roller though paint again as necessary.

3. Let paint dry. Print back of paper if desired.

4. Wash roller and paintbrush. Blot dry with paper towels. With marker, draw in sheep's features.

TO PRINT ON FABRIC:

1. Wash fabric to remove sizing. Press. Cover work surface with newspaper or plastic tablecloth.

2. Lay fabric flat on protected table surface. Tape down corners so fabric won't shift.

3. Mix fabric paint and spread a thin layer on tray. Run roller through paint and test print on a scrap of fabric. Print on fabric as you would on paper.

4. Let paint dry. To fix color, iron printed area according to manufacturer's directions.

THINGS TO MAKE FROM PRINTED PAPER

GIFT WRAP

Print on plain newsprint or white shelf paper to create wonderful and inexpensive wrapping paper. Shelf paper is available at grocery stores and at office supply stores (often as tablecloth covering).

GIFT BOW

YOU NEED:
- **Roller-printed paper (on both sides)**
- **Needle and thread**

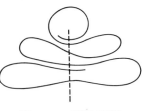

Diagram—GIFT BOW

TO MAKE:

1. Cut a strip of printed paper, 61 × 2.5 cm (24 × 1 in).

2. Bring end of strip up and over to form a loop approx 4.5 cm (1-3/4 in) wide, or half the size of the finished bow. Make a second loop the same size opposite

Colorful roller-printed items: (left to right) Ram Pillow (p. 55), Ewe Pillow (p. 54), Christmas Card (p. 52), assorted Packages (p. 52), Envelope (p. 52), Enclosure Card (p. 52) and Christmas Stickers (p. 52).

the first one. Folding back and forth, make another set of loops slightly smaller than the first, then make one small loop at centre top (see Diagram). Cut off any excess. Tuck cut end under so it is well hidden. To hold bow together, stitch through centre of loops. Knot thread ends at back of bow.

ENCLOSURE CARD

YOU NEED:
• **Unlined file card**
• **Co-ordinating strong thread**
• **Hole punch**

TO MAKE:
Fold file card in half. Print front and back with small motifs. As an alternative, cut a rectangle of printed paper and fold in half. Punch a hole near top inside corner of back of card. Slip a loop of thread through hole and make a knot, leaving ends long enough to tie to present.

CHRISTMAS CARD

YOU NEED:
• **Piece of paper, 28 × 18 cm (11 × 7 in)**
• **Piece of cardboard, 18 × 14 cm (7 × 5-1/2 in)**
• **Felt-tip marker**

TO MAKE:

1. Transfer solid outline of large or small sheep body (page 54 or page 50) onto centre of cardboard. Carefully cut along outline so you have both a cardboard sheep template and a rectangular stencil with a sheep cut out of the middle. Both patterns may be used.

2. Fold paper in half so short edges meet. Place sheep template (for printed surround) or stencil (for printed sheep and plain surround) on front of folded paper card. Print with plain or V-patterned roller. Remove template or stencil. Let paint dry.

3. With marker, draw in sheep's features. On inside of card, write a greeting — e.g., "We wish ewe a Merry Christmas."

ENVELOPE

YOU NEED:
• **Envelope**
• **Felt-tip marker**

TO MAKE:
Roll patterned roller with small sheep motif along left front edge of envelope so sheep run up the side. Let paint dry. Print the same on back of envelope. With marker, draw in sheep's features.

CHRISTMAS STICKERS

YOU NEED:
• **Self-adhesive labels, approx 10 × 5 cm (4 × 2 in), available at office supply stores**
• **Felt-tip marker**

TO MAKE:
Using plain roller, print over template or stencil of small sheep onto label (see Christmas Card, this page). Let paint dry. With marker, draw in sheep's features.

PACKAGES

Small box measures 6.5 cm (2-1/2 in) square, large box 12.5 cm (5 in) square. Small flat envelope package measures 15 × 10 cm (6 × 4 in), large one 30.5 × 20.5 cm (12 × 8 in). Small curved-end package measures 12.5 × 8 cm (5 × 3-1/8 in), large one 25.5 × 15 cm (10 × 6 in)

YOU NEED:
• **Roller-printed Bristol board or card stock**
• **White craft glue**
• **Geometry compass**
• **Ruler**
• **Brown paper**

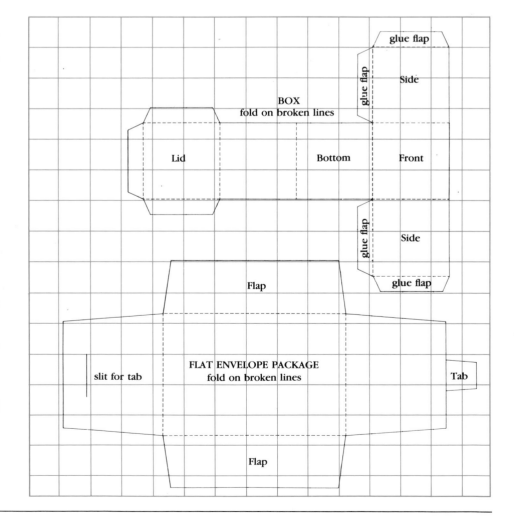

TO MAKE:

To enlarge package patterns, see General Directions (page 134), drawing grid lines 2.5 cm (1 in) apart for small packages, 5 cm (2 in) apart for large packages.

1. Trace outline of package pattern onto Bristol board or card. Cut out.

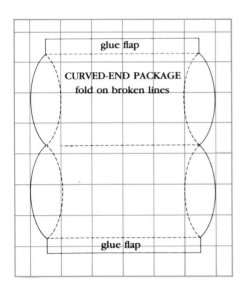

2. Mark fold lines indicated by broken lines on pattern. Using scissor blade, score along fold lines. Use edge of ruler as a guide on straight lines. This gives a clean, sharp fold.

3. On envelope package, cut slit in end flap. Fold up flaps and insert tab in slit. Fold up sides of box. Glue indicated flaps to inside of box. Fold curved-end package in half. Glue indicated flaps together on inside of package. When glue is dry, fold in curved end flaps.

PAPER CHAIN

YOU NEED:

• **Strip of paper approx 4.5 cm (1-3/4 in) wide × desired length of chain, roller-printed on both sides with small V motifs. For wider chain, cut strip 9 cm (3-1/2 in) wide.**
• **White craft glue**

TO MAKE:

Fold strip in half lengthwise. Fold wider chain in half again. Make cuts approx 1.5 cm (5/8 in) deep on alternate sides of folded strip every 6 mm (1/4 in). Unfold

Start an "ewe" tradition: trim your tree with Paper Chains, Sheep Chains and Lamb Ornaments.

and gently separate cuts. To make a longer chain, simply glue several strips together end to end.

SHEEP CHAIN

YOU NEED:

• **Strip of paper approx 12 cm (4-3/4 in) wide × desired length of chain, roller-printed on both sides with small V motifs**
• **Felt-tip marker**
• **Tracing paper**

TO MAKE:

1. Trace large sheep (with legs) (page 54) onto tracing paper following adjustments indicated by broken line.

2. Accordian pleat strip of paper so each pleat measures 10 cm (4 in) wide. Transfer outline of sheep onto top pleat so nose, chest and hind end are on folds. Cut out. Unfold chain.

3. With marker, draw in sheep's features.

THINGS TO MAKE FROM PRINTED FABRIC

LAMB ORNAMENT

YOU NEED:

• **Piece of roller-printed fabric, 23 × 12.5 cm (9 × 5 in)**
• **.30 m double-fold bias tape**
• **Embroidery floss**
• **Small amount of polyester fibrefill**

TO MAKE:

1. Fold fabric in half so right sides are together and short edges meet. Trace around large sheep template (see Christmas Card, Step 1) onto folded fabric. Cut out, leaving a 6 mm (1/4-in) seam allowance on all edges.

2. Topstitch long edges of bias tape together. Cut four 4 cm (1-5/8-in) lengths for legs, one 7.5 cm (3-in) length for tail and one 5 cm (2-in) length for ears.

3. With raw edges even, baste one end of legs to right side of one body piece as indicated on pattern. Knot one end of tail. Baste other end to body as for legs.

4. With right sides together, sew body pieces together using a 6 mm seam allowance and leaving open between legs. Clip curves. Turn right side out. Press. Stuff firmly. Slipstitch opening closed.

5. With floss, embroider eyes, nose and mouth. Fold ear bias tape so raw ends meet at centre point. Take a few stitches at centre to secure. Having seam on underside, slipstitch ears across top of sheep's head.

6. Thread hanging loop of floss through top of sheep.

EWE PILLOW

YOU NEED:
- **Piece of roller-printed fabric, 61 × 43 cm (24 × 17 in)**
- **.90 m wide double-fold bias tape**
- **Embroidery floss**
- **2 beads, 6 mm in diameter**
- **Polyester fibrefill**
- **Brown paper**

TO MAKE:

To enlarge large *sheep pattern, see General Directions (page 134).*

1. Topstitch long edges of bias tape together. Cut four 11.5 cm (4-1/2-in) lengths for legs, one 18 cm (7-in) length for tail and two 9 cm (3-1/2-in) lengths for ears.

2. Cut out and assemble as for Lamb Ornament (above).

A Ewe Pillow sewn from roller-printed fabric.

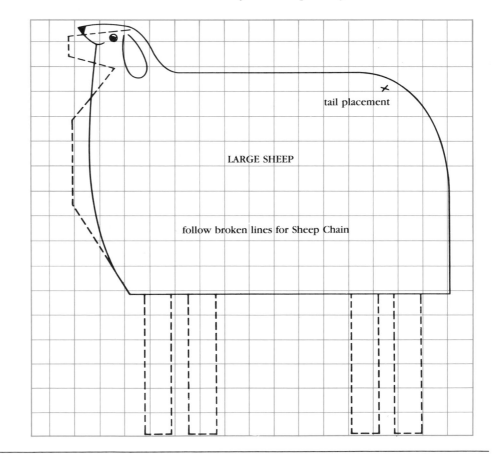

tail placement

LARGE SHEEP

follow broken lines for Sheep Chain

3. Sew on beads for eyes. Embroider mouth and nose. Fold each piece of bias tape for ears in half so raw ends meet. Stitch ends together. Turn loops right side out. Slipstitch in place on either side of head.

RAM PILLOW

YOU NEED:
- **Piece of roller-printed fabric, 106.5 × 61 cm (42 × 24 in)**
- **1.30 m wide double-fold bias tape**
- **Embroidery floss**
- **2 buttons, 10 mm in diameter**
- **Polyester fibrefill**
- **Brown paper**

TO MAKE:
To enlarge small *sheep pattern, see General Directions (page 134), drawing grid lines 7.5 cm (3 in) apart.*

1. Topstitch long edges of bias tape together. Cut four 12.5 cm (5-in) lengths for legs, one 23 cm (9-in) length for tail and two 24 cm (9-1/2-in) lengths for horns.

2. Cut out and assemble as for Ewe Pillow (previous page).

3. Sew on buttons for eyes. Embroider mouth and nose. Roll end of each piece of bias tape for horns into a 2.5 cm (1-in) diameter circle. With opposite end, roll a larger circle around the smaller one. Tack circles together with a few stitches and slipstitch in place behind each eye.

CHILD'S PLAY SMOCK

(ages 4 to 7)

YOU NEED:
- **.70 m polyester/cotton fabric, 115 cm wide**
- **Piece of roller-printed fabric, 15 × 12.5 cm (6 × 5 in)**
- **Piece of fusible interfacing, 15 × 12.5 cm**
- **2 m wide double-fold bias tape**
- **.35 m narrow double-fold bias tape**
- **Matching threads**
- **Embroidery floss**
- **Dressmaker's chalk**

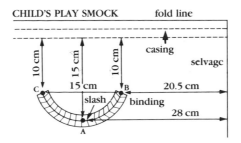

CHILD'S PLAY SMOCK — fold line — casing — selvage — 10 cm — 15 cm — 10 cm — 15 cm — 20.5 cm — 28 cm — C — B — slash — binding — A

TO MAKE:

1. Press under 6 mm (1/4 in), then 4.5 cm (1-3/4 in) along one long edge of polyester/cotton fabric. Stitch close to first fold then 1.5 cm (5/8 in) from this to form casing.

2. Following measurements shown on Diagram, mark points A, B and C. Join these 3 points with a curved line. Cut along curved line for armhole. Cut two 21.5 cm (8-1/2-in) lengths of wide bias tape. Bind upper and lower edges of armhole with this tape, turning under raw ends as you go. Reinforce stitching at ends. Repeat for opposite armhole.

3. Fuse interfacing to wrong side of printed fabric. Trace around large sheep template (see Christmas Card, Step 1) onto fabric. Cut out. Pin sheep to front of smock where desired approx 19 cm (7-1/2 in) from bottom.

4. Topstitch long edges of narrow bias tape together. Cut five 4 cm (1-5/8-in) lengths for legs and ear, and one 5 cm (2-in) length for tail. Pin tail and legs in place, tucking raw ends under body. Fold ear bias tape in half so raw ends meet. Tuck raw ends under body where indicated for ear. Fold ear down toward face. Machine satin-stitch around sheep's body. With floss, embroider a French knot for eye.
For ram's horn, omit ear. Cut a 9 cm (3-1/2-in) length of narrow bias tape. Shape an inner and outer circle as for Ram Pillow (this page). Slipstitch to head.

5. Hem smock to desired length.

6. Topstitch long edge of remaining wide bias tape together. Thread through neck casing. Knot at both ends. Pull up and adjust gathers.

A roller-printed ram accents this Child's Play Smock.

GIFTS FOR LITTLE HANDS TO MAKE

Nothing is more rewarding to a child than being able to say "... and I made it myself!" With a bit of encouragement and an assortment of simple household materials, even little hands can produce presents such as a Tissue-Paper Tree, a Candy-Cane Reindeer and Mouse-In-A-Bed ornaments that family, friends and teachers will adore.

DESIGNS BY SALLY MEDLAND

STRAWBERRY ORNAMENT

Paint a whole walnut with shiny red paint. When paint dries, dab on dots of glue with toothpick and glue tiny white seed beads in place. Glue a loop of gold thread to top of strawberry. Cut out green leaves from scraps of felt. Glue leaves to top of strawberry.

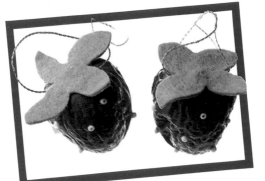

CANDY-CANE REINDEER

Twist a long colored pipe cleaner around top of candy cane. Bend ends into shape of funny antlers. Glue on a little red pom-pom nose and 2 rolly eyes. Tie fancy bow around neck.

Strawberry Ornaments.

TISSUE-PAPER SNOWMAN AND TREE

Cut out a Christmas shape, such as a Christmas tree, a snowman or a wreath from cardboard. Cut colored tissue paper into many 5 cm (2-in) squares. Fold each square over pointer finger and scrunch together at fingertip. Glue to cardboard so shape is completely covered. Decorate tree with little red tissue-paper balls or pom-poms for berries or white balls for snowflakes. Decorate snowman with pipe cleaner or paper bow and paper hat. Trim wreath with paper bow and berries.

MOUSE-IN-A-BED ORNAMENT

With a marker, draw a mouse face on a hazelnut. Cut mouse ears from colored felt and glue them to each side of hazelnut head. Glue a loop of thread inside a half walnut shell. Glue a piece of elastic band at pointed end of walnut shell for mouse tail. Glue hazelnut head to other end of walnut shell. Dab glue around inside edge of walnut. Poke little piece of fabric into shell to cover up mouse. Hang on tree with loop of thread.

REINDEER GIFT TAG

Cut a small diamond from construction paper. Fold in half to make a triangle. Cut 2 holly-shaped antlers from green paper and glue to top of triangle head along fold. Draw 2 eyes with marker and glue on a tiny red pom-pom nose.

DUCK ORNAMENT

Gather together little scraps of wood, wood bits from craft store or cut pieces of cardboard into different shapes. Paint with bright Christmassy-colored acrylic paint. Place on waxed paper to dry. Glue together into shape of duck. Decorate with ribbon. Glue wire Christmas tree hanger to back.

Mice in their beds.

Reindeer Gift Tags.

Tissue-Paper Snowman (at top) and Tree (above).

Duck Ornament.   *Candy-Cane Reindeer.*

COOKIE-CUTTER CHRISTMAS

Simple cookie-cutter shapes are the starting point for delightful projects for children. Some of them can be made by children — with a little help from you. Cookie-Time Accessories, Paper Chains, Appliquéd Napkins and Stuffed Shapes are all quick and easy gift ideas that can involve the whole family. You can produce the Gingerbread Boy and Girl Cloth Dolls, Tree Skirt, Crib Quilt, Appliquéd Bib and Child's Pullover to continue the youthful theme.

DESIGNS BY MARY CORCORAN

Create a marvelous collection of treasures using any cookie cutters you may have on hand.

COOKIE-TIME ACCESSORIES

Trace around cookie cutters onto adhesive paper. Cut out shapes and stick onto a wooden basket, a paper gift bag or a clear acrylic cookie jar filled with cutout cookies, onto clear plastic glasses or a plastic place mat.

APPLIQUÉD NAPKIN

Use a purchased cloth napkin or hem a 36 cm (14-1/4-in) square of desired fabric. Iron lightweight fusible interfacing to back of scrap (approx size of cookie cutter motif) of colored broadcloth. This gives broadcloth more body and makes appliquéing easier. Trace around cookie cutter onto back of interfaced scrap. Cut out. Position appliqué on corner of napkin. Machine satin-stitch in place around outline of shape. Decorate with ribbon bow if appropriate.

PAPER CHAINS

Use colored tissue paper for lightweight chain to hang as a garland (it's easy to cut many layers at one time). For stiffer chain that stands up, use fewer layers of construction paper.

Diagram—PAPER CHAIN

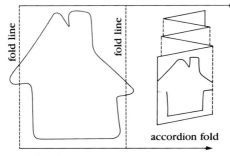

TO MAKE:

1. Cut paper into a long strip × height of cookie cutter. Trace around cookie cutter onto one end of strip so that outline of shape extends 6 mm (1/4 in) beyond end of paper (see Diagram).

2. Accordion-fold strip so outline of shape extends 6 mm beyond folds at each side. Fold as many layers as you can comfortably cut at a time.

3. Cut along outline of shape. Open out

chain. For long chain, make several strips and glue together.

STUFFED SHAPES

1. For small shapes, trace around cookie cutter onto interfaced fabric, and cut out 2 of each shape, leaving a 6 mm (1/4 -in) seam allowance.
For pillow size, enlarge cookie cutter shape as follows: Trace around cookie cutter onto paper. Draw a grid of horizontal and vertical lines 1 cm (3/8 in) apart on top of outline. Draw an enlarged grid on brown paper with lines approx 3 to 4 cm (1-1/4 to 1-1/2 in) apart. Enlarge outline following General Directions (page 134). Pattern may also be enlarged photostatically, 300 to 400 percent. Cut out 2 enlarged shapes from interfaced fabric.

2. With right sides together, stitch shapes together using a 6 mm seam allowance and leaving a small opening along one edge. Clip corners and curves. Turn right side out. Stuff with fibrefill. Slipstitch opening closed.

3. Thread hanging loop through top of small shapes for tree ornaments or sew them in a row for a three-dimensional garland.

CHILD'S YOKED PULLOVER

Pullover is worked on circular needles in one piece to armholes. Sleeves are knitted separately, then joined to body at beginning of yoke. Fair Isle design is knitted into pullover; gingerbread men and heart motifs are embroidered on when complete. Recommended for beginner knitters with some experience. Instructions are written for size 2. Any changes for sizes 4, 6 and 8 are written in brackets.

YOU NEED:
- **Patons Canadiana Sayelle (50 g balls) in the following colors and quantities: 3 (4, 5, 5) white, MC 1 ball each of contrasting colors: Green (B), Blue (C), Yellow (D) and Red (E)**
- **One 3.75 mm circular needle, 60 cm long (40 cm long for size 2)**
- **One 4.50 mm circular needle, 60 cm long (40 cm long for size 2)**
- **Four 3.75 mm double-pointed needles**
- **Four 4.50 mm double-pointed needles OR whichever needles you require to produce the tension given below**
- **4 stitch holders**
- **Tapestry needle**
- **Tracing paper**
- **Water-soluble fabric marker**

Tension:
20 sts and 26 rows = 10 cm (4 ins) in St st using larger needles. Work to the exact tension with the specified yarn to obtain satisfactory results.
TO SAVE TIME, TAKE TIME TO CHECK TENSION.

TO MAKE:
See General Directions (page 134) for knitting abbreviations.
Note: Work knit-in design by carrying MC loosely across back (wrong side) of work but never over more than 3 sts. When it must pass over more than 3 sts, weave it over and under color in use on next st or at centre of sts it passes over. When changing colors, in order to prevent a hole, pass color to be used under and around to right of color just used.

BODY
With MC and smaller circular needle, cast on 116 (120, 128, 140) sts. Join in rnd and place a marker on first st. Work in (k1, p1) ribbing for 5 cm (2 ins). Change to larger circular needle and k 1 rnd.

CHILD'S YOKED PULLOVER

Sizes:	2	4	6	8
Chest measurement:	53 cm (21 ins)	56 cm (22 ins)	61 cm (24 ins)	66 cm (26 ins)
Finished chest measurement:	58 cm (23 ins)	61 cm (24 ins)	66 cm (26 ins)	71 cm (28 ins)
Length at centre back:	32 cm (12-1/2 ins)	34 cm (13-1/2 ins)	38 cm (15 ins)	39 cm (15-1/2 ins)
Sleeve length to underarm:	24 cm (9-1/2 ins)	27 cm (10-1/2 ins)	29 cm (11-1/2 ins)	33 cm (13 ins)

Children will love to wear these cosy Yoked Pullovers.

Work from Graph 1 to end of graph, reading rows from right to left.
With MC, continue to k in rnds until work from beg measures 19 (20, 24, 25) cm/ 7-1/2 (8, 9-1/2, 9-3/4) ins or desired length to underarm.
Next rnd: K5. Sl these sts and 4 (4, 4, 5) sts from end of previous rnd onto a st holder for armhole. K58 (60, 64, 70) sts. Sl last 9 (9, 9, 10) sts just worked onto a st holder for armhole. K to end of rnd. Do not break yarn.

SLEEVES

With MC and smaller double-pointed needles, cast on 28 (32, 34, 34) sts. Divide these sts onto 3 needles. Join in rnd and place a marker on first st. Work in (k1, p1) ribbing for 6 cm (2-1/4 ins) inc 2 sts evenly across last rnd for sizes 6 and 8 only. 28 (32, 36, 36) sts now on needle. Change to larger double-pointed needles and k 1 rnd.
Work from Graph 1 to end of graph, reading rows from right to left.
With MC, continue to k in rnds, inc 1 st

CHILD'S PULLOVER

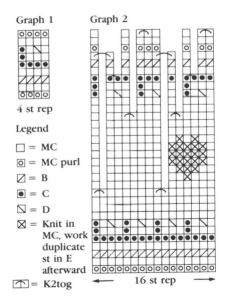

Graph 1   Graph 2

4 st rep

Legend

☐ = MC
◉ = MC purl
◿ = B
⬤ = C
◹ = D
⊠ = Knit in MC, work duplicate st in E afterward
⟁ = K2tog

← 16 st rep →

at beg and end of next, then every following 6th rnd until there are 40 (46, 50, 54) sts on needle.
Continue even until sleeve from beg measures 24 (27, 29, 33) cm/9-1/2 (10-1/2, 11-1/2, 13) ins or desired length to underarm.
Next rnd: K5. Sl these sts and 4 (4, 4, 5) sts from end of previous rnd onto a st holder. Break yarn, leaving an end 30 cm

GINGERBREAD MAN MOTIF

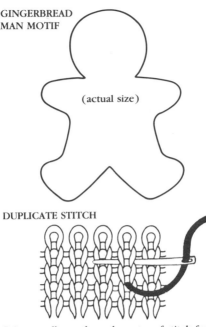

(actual size)

DUPLICATE STITCH

Bring needle up through centre of stitch from back of work, insert from right to left behind stitch immediately above, then down through centre of original stitch and out through centre of next stitch to be worked.

SPLIT STITCH

(12 ins) long for grafting at underarm. Place remaining sts on a thread.

YOKE

With MC and larger circular needle, k across sts of one sleeve, first body section, second sleeve and second body section. 160 (176, 192, 208) sts in rnd. Mark last stitch as end of rnd.
Size 2: K 0 rnds.
Sizes 4 and 6: K 1 rnd.
Size 8: K 2 rnds.

Note: To accommodate dec in sts, it may be necessary for some sizes to change to set of double-pointed needles to complete graph.
All sizes: Work Graph 2 to end of graph, reading rows from right to left and marking st at bottom point of each heart motif with colored thread. 60 (66, 72, 78) sts in rnd.

NECKBAND

With MC and smaller double-pointed needles, work in (k1, p1) ribbing for 5 cm (2 ins).
Change to larger double-pointed needles and rib 2 rnds. Cast off loosely in ribbing.

TO FINISH:

1. Fold neckband in half to wrong side and slipstitch cast-off edge loosely to first row of ribbing.

2. With E, work heart motifs around yoke in duplicate st. Trace gingerbread man motif onto tracing paper and cut out. Using fabric marker, trace around pattern (centred between Fair Isle bands and each heart motif) onto yoke of pullover. With tapestry needle and B, embroider outline of man in split stitch.

3. Graft underarms as follows:
Line up sts on 2 double-pointed needles, holding them parallel with right side of work facing.
Thread tapestry needle with length of yarn and, working from right to left, rep the following steps until all sts on both needles have been eliminated.
*Thread needle knitways through first st on front needle, draw yarn through and sl st off needle. Thread through next st on front needle purlways, draw yarn through and leave st on needle. Take yarn under needle and thread purlways into first st on back needle, draw yarn through and sl st off needle. Thread knitways into next st on back needle, draw yarn through and leave st on needle. Bring yarn forward under needle and rep from *.

TREE SKIRT

YOU NEED:

- .80 m felt, 180 cm wide, for background
- .50 m contrasting colored felt, 180 cm wide, for border
- Small pieces of felt in assorted colors, for appliqués
- Thread to match border

• .80 m polyester fleece, for backing
• **Geometry compass**
• **White craft glue**

TO MAKE:

1. Press fabrics. Cut an 80 cm (31-1/2-in) square from background felt and from fleece. Pin squares together. Locate centre point by folding square in half one way, then the other. At centre of square, draw a circle with an 8 cm (3-1/4-in) radius. Also draw a line for slit, from centre point to midpoint along one edge of square. Pin layers together around circle and on each side of slit line. Cut out circle and along slit line.

2. Cut 3 strips of border felt 6 cm (2-1/4-in) × width of fabric. Fold each strip in half so long edges meet. Press. Pin folded border around all edges of square, along both edges of slit and around centre circle (cutting at each corner), completely encasing raw edges. Zigzag close to cut edges of border through all layers. Trace around cookie cutters onto colored felt. Cut out shapes and glue to tree skirt as desired.

GINGERBREAD BOY AND GIRL CLOTH DOLLS

YOU NEED (for each doll):
• **Piece of broadcloth, 60 × 45 cm (23-5/8 × 17-3/4 in), for body**
• **Square of white broadcloth 10 cm (4 in), for face**
• **Pieces of broadcloth in assorted colors, for clothes**
• **Piece of polyester fleece, 60 × 45 cm**
• **Lightweight fusible interfacing**
• **Matching threads**
• **Embroidery floss**
• **2 Velcro dot fasteners**
• **Geometry compass**
• **Water-soluble fabric marker**
• **Brown paper**
• **Tracing paper**

TO MAKE:
To enlarge doll patterns, see General Directions (page 134).

1. Cut 2 doll shapes from broadcloth and 2 from fleece.

2. Iron interfacing to back of white

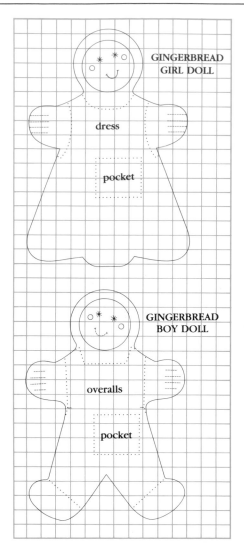

GINGERBREAD GIRL DOLL

dress

pocket

GINGERBREAD BOY DOLL

overalls

pocket

broadcloth square. With compass, draw a 9 cm (3-1/2-in) circle on square (face). Using 3 strands of floss, embroider star eyes, mouth (running stitches) and cheeks (chain stitch in a circle). Cut out face. Pin to right side of head at a slight angle. Machine satin-stitch in place around edge.

3. Place doll front and back, right sides together, on top of 2 layers of fleece. Pin. Stitch all layers together using a 6 mm (1/4-in) seam allowance, leaving a 5 cm (2-in) opening along one side of body. Trim away excess fleece. Trim seam allowance. Clip corners and curves. Turn right side out. Press. Stuff hands lightly. Topstitch finger lines. Stuff rest of body firmly. Slipstitch opening closed.

4. **Hair:** Cut 1.5 cm (5/8-in) wide bias strips from broadcloth. Wrap strips around a 20 × 6 cm (7-7/8- × 2-3/8-in) piece of paper, overlapping slightly. Zigzag lengthwise down centre of paper.

Tear away paper. Twist loops to look like curls. Stitch to top of doll's head.

5. **Girl's dress:** Trace dotted dress pattern lines onto tracing paper. Add 13 mm (1/2 in) to all edges. Cut out paper pattern. From dress fabric, cut out 1 dress front. Fold pattern in half lengthwise (dress back pattern) and cut 2 backs from dress fabric, adding 2 cm (3/4 in) to *straight* edges only.

With right sides together and using a 6 mm seam allowance, stitch front to backs at shoulders and sides. Press seams open. Turn under 6 mm, then 6 mm again, down centre back edges. Hem.

Cut a strip of broadcloth 115 × 8 cm (45 × 3-1/8 in) for hem ruffle. Hem short ends. Fold in half so wrong sides are together and long edges meet. Press. Run a gathering thread down long raw edge, 6 mm from edge. Pull up thread. With right sides together, pin raw edge of ruffle to hem edge. Gather evenly. Stitch using a 6 mm seam allowance. Press ruffle down. Topstitch seam allowance 3 mm (1/8 in) from seam.

Cut a strip of broadcloth 80 × 8 cm (31-1/2 × 3-1/8 in) for neck ruffle. Hem short ends. Gather and stitch to neck edge as for hem ruffle. Sew Velcro fasteners to either side of back opening. Trace dotted pocket lines onto tracing paper. Add 13 mm to all edges. Cut out paper pattern. Cut pocket from desired fabric. Iron interfacing to back of pocket. Turn under 13 mm on all edges. Topstitch top edge. Topstitch remaining 3 edges in place on dress.

Cut 2 strips 24 × 3 cm (9-1/2 × 1-1/8 in) for armhole binding. With right sides together, stitch one raw edge of binding around armhole. Cut off any excess length. Stitch ends together. Turn under 6 mm along remaining raw edge. Fold binding to inside and hem.

6. **Boy's overalls:** Trace dotted overall lines onto tracing paper. Add 13 mm to all edges. Cut out paper pattern. From overall fabric, cut 2 overall pieces. Turn under 6 mm at armholes, shoulders and neck. Turn under 13 mm at leg hems. Satin-stitch over raw edges. With right sides together and using a 6 mm seam allowance, sew front to back at sides and inseam. Clip corners. Turn right side out. Sew Velcro dot fasteners at shoulders.

Gingerbread Boy and Girl Cloth Dolls go hand in hand.

Assemble and apply pocket to overalls as for dress. Cut a 10 cm (4-in) square of broadcloth for hankie. Hem. Tuck into pocket.

For neckerchief pattern, draw a 27 cm (10-5/8-in) square on paper. Cut out, then cut in half diagonally. Using this triangular pattern, cut 1 neckerchief from broadcloth. Hem. Tie around doll's neck.

Tuck baby in under this terrific Crib Quilt or use it to decorate the wall of the nursery.

CRIB QUILT

Finished crib quilt measures approx 148 × 88 cm (58-1/4 × 34-5/8 in).

YOU NEED:
- **2.60 m cotton/polyester broadcloth, 115 cm wide, for quilt top and backing**
- **1.75 m contrasting colored cotton/ polyester broadcloth, 115 cm wide, for border**
- **Small pieces of broadcloth in assorted colors, sizes of desired appliqué motifs**
- **Lightweight fusible interfacing**
- **Matching threads**
- **Embroidery floss**
- **Quilting thread**
- **Quilt batting**
- **Water-soluble fabric marker**

TO MAKE:

1. From longest length of broadcloth, cut 1 rectangle for quilt top and 1 for quilt backing, each 130 × 70 cm (51 × 27-1/2 in).

2. **Quilt top:** Interface and cut out desired small appliqué shapes as for napkin (page 59). For large appliqués, assemble *front* only of gingerbread boy and girl body and clothes without fleece lining (page 62). Iron interfacing to wrong side of each. Pin appliqués to quilt top in desired position or use photo as a guide. Machine satin-stitch in place.

3. **Borders:** Cut 2 strips of border fabric 70 × 23 cm (27-1/2 × 9 in). Using a 13 mm (1/2-in) seam allowance, stitch strips to top and bottom edges of quilt top. Press.
Cut another 2 strips 180 × 23 cm (71 × 9 in). Stitch these strips to each side edge of quilt top. Press. Trim away excess fabric at ends.
With *right sides together*, centre one short end of backing rectangle along one short end of quilt top as shown in Diagram. Stitch.

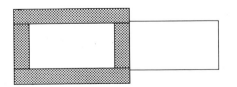

Stitch other end of backing to other end

of quilt top in same manner. Now centre and stitch long edges of backing to sides of quilt top in same manner, leaving a 40 cm (15-3/4-in) opening at centre of one side. Press quilt flat to create neatly folded borders around all sides of quilt.

4. **Corners:** Pinch together fabric at each corner. Draw a line from each corner of central rectangle on quilt top to outer corner of border. Stitch along each marked line. Trim seam allowance. Turn right side out through opening. Press.

5. **Quilting lines:** Using fabric marker, trace around desired cookie cutters onto borders for quilting motifs. Measuring from centre outward in both directions, mark lines 5 cm (2 in) apart across central rectangle on quilt top.

6. Lay quilt on top of batting. Cut batting to this size. Insert batting into quilt through opening, smoothing out all wrinkles. Slipstitch opening closed. Baste from centre to corners and to midpoint along each side.

7. With appropriate color of thread, quilt around all appliquéd shapes and along all marked lines. Wipe off lines.

APPLIQUÉD BIB

Use a purchased terry cloth baby bib or make one from a large facecloth as follows: Mark centre point along one short edge of facecloth. Measure and mark points 4.5 cm (1-3/4 in) to right and left of this point and a third point 9 cm (3-1/2 in) in towards centre of facecloth. Join latter 3 points with a curved line to form rounded neck opening. Cut out neck. Bind straight edges with extra-wide, double-fold bias tape. Bind neck edge with another length of bias tape leaving 30 cm (11-3/4 in) extending at each corner of neck for ties. Stitch edges of tie tape together.
Cut out appliqué shapes from interfaced broadcloth and satin-stitch to bib as for napkin (page 59).

Appliquéd fabric shapes make a plain terry Bib look irresistible.

Canadian Living

GLORIOUS CHRISTMAS CRAFTS

HEIRLOOM TREASURES

CHAPTER IV

TREETOP ANGEL

Create an exquisite angel to adorn the top of your tree for years to come. Golden threads highlight the moiré taffeta, an antique lace doily with crocheted edgings forms the wings and the delicate face is embroidered with floss. A work of art this special is sure to become a family heirloom.

DESIGN BY CAROL SCHMIDT

YOU NEED:

- **Piece of white moiré taffeta, 30 × 21 cm (11-7/8 × 8-1/4 in)**
- **Piece of white felt, 30 × 21 cm**
- **Scrap of flesh-tone felt**
- **White crocheted doily with fluted edge, approx 17 cm (6-3/4 in) in diameter**
- **Silk or viscose embroidery floss, peach and dark coral**
- **DMC embroidery floss:**
   No. 931 — grey-blue
   No. 732 — olive
   No. 938 — dark brown
   No. 498 — red
- **DMC Fil Or (gold)**
- **Gold lamé yarn**
- **No. 10 white crochet cotton**
- **No. 8 white DMC coton perlé**
- **White and flesh-tone sewing thread**
- **Embroidery hoop, 30 cm in diameter**
- **Muslin to fit hoop**
- **Embroidery needle**
- **2.00 mm and 3.00 mm crochet hooks**
- **Small artist's paintbrush**
- **Powder blush**

TO MAKE:

For crochet abbreviations and to enlarge angel pattern, see General Directions (page 134). Refer to Embroidery Diagram for embroidery stitches.

1. Cut 2 angel shapes from taffeta, for front and back and 2 from felt, for liner. Cut face and hands from flesh-tone felt.

2. Stretch muslin in hoop. Baste one taffeta piece (front of angel) to muslin.

3. Sew felt face to front, using tiny backstitches. With a single strand of floss and small outline stitches, embroider brown eyes and red mouth. Fill in mouth with small straight stitches.

4. With Fil Or, work spaced blanket stitches around edge of face, varying the length of the stitches to shape halo. Starting at edge of face with same thread, weave over and under blanket stitches, going through fabric only at each end of halo. Continue weaving back and forth around face, packing weaving solid until halo is filled.
With same thread, embroider 3-petal flowers around edge of halo using detached chain stitch.

5. With 3 strands of peach floss, embroider French knots, closely spaced around edge of face, wrapping floss 3 times around needle for each knot.

6. With Fil Or, stem-stitch inner and outer lines of dress. Chain-stitch bottom line of yoke.

7. With a single strand of dark coral floss, fill yoke with laid thread work. Following Laid Thread Diagram, tack down laid threads with crosses (using single strand of grey-blue floss) and French knots (using 4 strands of olive floss).

8. With Fil Or, embroider centre panel as shown.

9. Working from inside to outside edge with Fil Or, fill in side panels of dress between stem-stitch outlines with the following row sequence: 1 row chain stitch, 1 row slanted feather stitch, 1 row chain stitch, *3 rows closely spaced stem stitch, 1 row chain stitch. Repeat from * until area is completely filled.

10. Sew on felt hands using tiny backstitches.

11. Remove muslin/taffeta from hoop. With right sides of taffeta together, stitch front to back using a 6 mm (1/4-in) seam allowance, leaving bottom edge open. Turn right side out.

12. Stitch felt liner pieces together using a 10 mm (3/8-in) seam allowance, leaving bottom edge open. Trim seam allowance close to stitching. With wrong sides together, fit liner inside taffeta angel. Turn under 6 mm around bottom edge on both fabrics. With coton perlé, buttonhole stitch the edges together, making stitches 3 mm (1/8 in) apart.

13. Lower hem fringe: With smaller crochet hook and crochet cotton, work in rounds as follows:
Rnd 1: Work 2 dc in each blanket stitch along bottom edge, join to first dec with sl st.
Rnd 2: *Sk 1 st, 5 dc in next st (this forms shell). Rep from * to end of rnd.
Rnd 3: Sl st in first 3 sts of first shell, ch 5, *1 sc in third dc of next shell, ch 5 (this forms bar). Rep from * to end of rnd, sl st in third sl st at beg of rnd to join.
Rnd 4: Sl st in first 2 sts of bar, 1 sc around same bar, 5 dc in sc, *1 sc around next bar, 5 dc in next sc. Rep from * to end of rnd.
Rnd 5: As Rnd 3.
Rnd 6: Sl st in first 2 sts of bar, 1 sc around same bar, ch 5, *1 sc around next bar, ch 5. Rep from * to end of rnd and join to first sc with sl st.
Rnd 7: Work 7 dc into each bar of previous rnd, join to first dc with sl st.
Rnd 8: As Rnd 2. Fasten off and weave in yarn end.

14. **Upper hem fringe**: With smaller crochet hook and gold lamé yarn, work upper fringe on top of lower fringe as follows:
Rnd 1: Work 2 sc in each blanket stitch

along bottom edge, working one on each side of 2 dc that were worked in first rnd of crochet cotton fringe. Join to first sc with sl st.

Rnds 2 to 4: Work as given for lower hem fringe, working 4 dc instead of 5 dc in sc in Rnd. 4.

15. **Wings:** Fold doily in half. With larger crochet hook and gold lamé yarn, sc along curved edge through both layers of doily being careful to keep work flat. Ch 3, turn.

Row 2: Dc to end of row, turn.

Row 3: *Sk 1 st, work 5 dc in next st. Rep from * to end of row. Fasten off and weave in yarn end.

With straight edge at top, tack wings to back of angel at centre point and at side edges.

16. Using paintbrush, highlight cheeks with a little blush.

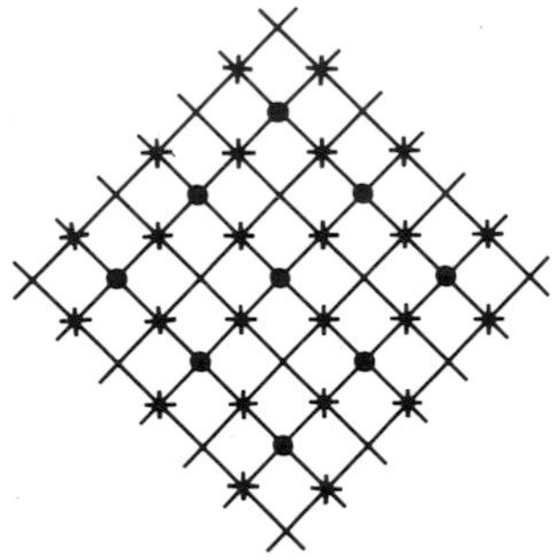

LAID THREAD DIAGRAM

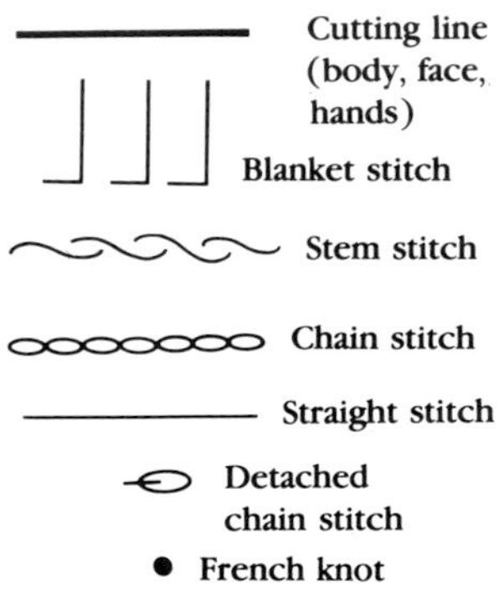
Cutting line (body, face, hands)
Blanket stitch
Stem stitch
Chain stitch
Straight stitch
Detached chain stitch
French knot

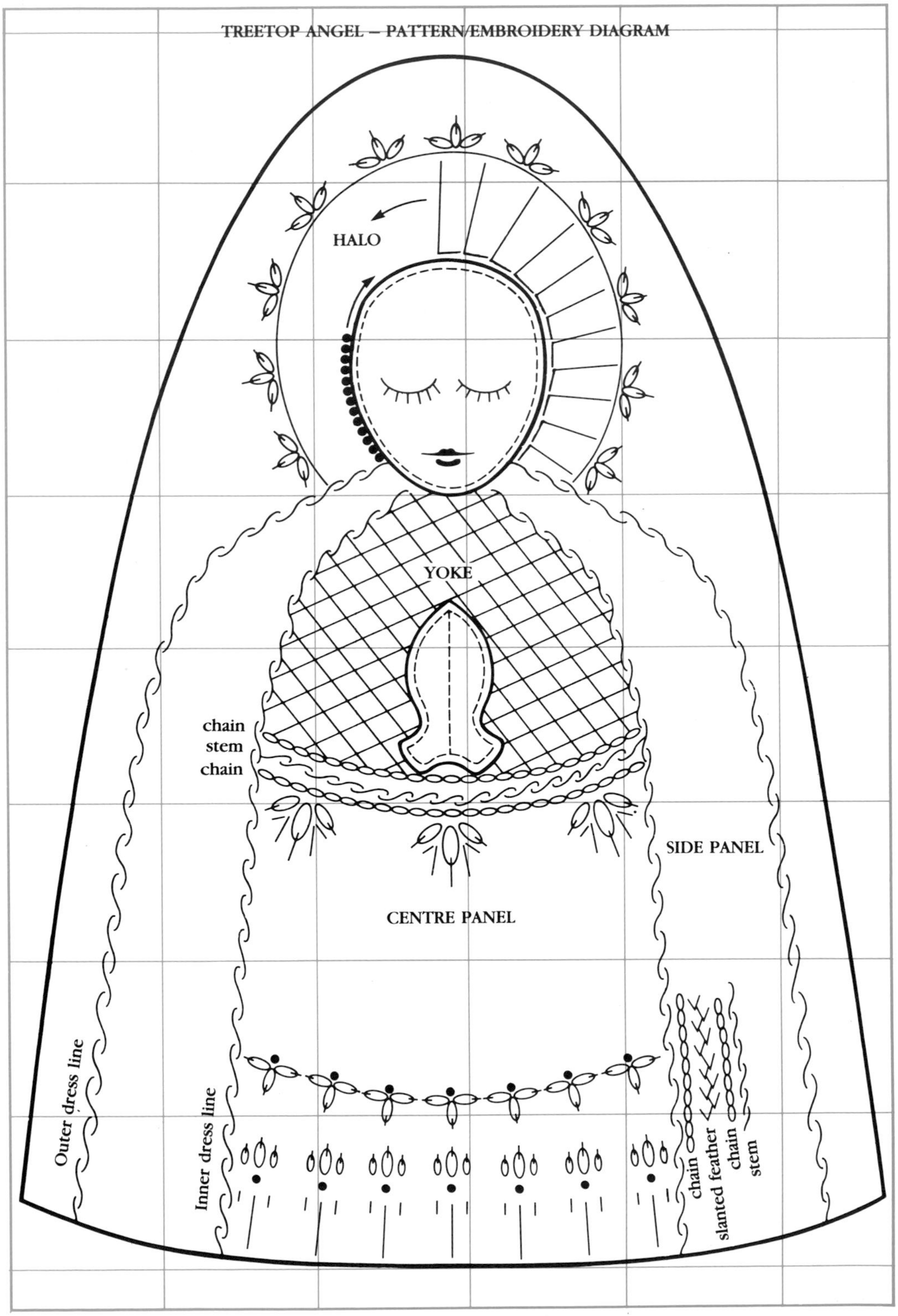
TREETOP ANGEL – PATTERN/EMBROIDERY DIAGRAM
HALO
YOKE
chain
stem
chain
SIDE PANEL
CENTRE PANEL
Outer dress line
Inner dress line
chain
slanted feather
chain
stem

SANTA AND MRS. CLAUS

Christmas just wouldn't be complete without a visit from jolly Santa and Mrs. Claus. Here is the most adorable little pair imaginable. Let them preside over your holiday festivities and bring the happy spirit of Christmas into your home.

DESIGN BY MARGARET STEPHENSON COOLE

The finished dolls are approx 30 cm (11-7/8 in) tall.

YOU NEED:

For both dolls:

- .50 m flesh-tone broadcloth, 115 cm wide
- .20 m red-and-white-striped cotton, 115 cm wide
- Matching threads
- Buttonhole twist thread, flesh-tone and navy blue
- Red embroidery floss
- 4 navy-blue buttons, 7 mm in diameter
- 4 clear beads, 4 mm in diameter
- Small amount of white washed sheep's fleece (available at weaving supply stores)
- Doll-making needle
- Embroidery needle
- Pink colored pencil
- Polyester fibrefill
- Spray starch
- Brown paper

For both dolls' clothes:

- .60 m red velveteen, 115 cm wide
- .40 m red broadcloth, 115 cm wide
- .20 m polka-dot cotton fabric, 115 cm wide
- .20 m white woven-stripe cotton fabric, 115 cm wide
- .30 m white woven-check cotton fabric, 115 cm wide
- .20 m red-and-white-striped knit fabric, 150 cm wide
- Piece of white short-pile fake fur, 35 × 12 cm (13-7/8 × 4-3/4 in)
- Piece of black felt, 30 cm (11-7/8 in) square
- Scrap of red felt
- .70 m white pre-gathered lace,

40 mm wide
- .40 m white pre-gathered lace, 20 mm wide
- .50 m white pre-gathered lace, 10 mm wide
- .70 m white flat lace, 10 mm wide
- .20 m red satin ribbon, 3 mm wide
- .30 m black velvet ribbon, 6 mm wide
- .30 m black braided piping, 15 mm wide
- 1 m narrow red cord
- .40 m black twill tape, 10 mm wide

- .60 m white elastic, 6 mm wide
- .30 m white elastic, 3 mm wide
- .20 m black elastic, 6 mm wide
- 2 black beads, 4 mm in diameter
- 8 red beads, 4 mm in diameter
- 4 red buttons, 10 mm in diameter
- 10 black snap fasteners, 5 mm in diameter
- 4 jingle bells
- Geometry compass

TO MAKE:

To enlarge patterns for dolls and clothes, see General Directions (page 134).

Note: Cut velveteen so direction of nap runs from top to bottom of each piece. Use closely spaced machine stitches and a 6 mm (1/4-in) seam allowance throughout, unless otherwise indicated. Backstitch at the beginning and end of all seams.

DOLLS

1. **For Santa:** From flesh-tone broadcloth,

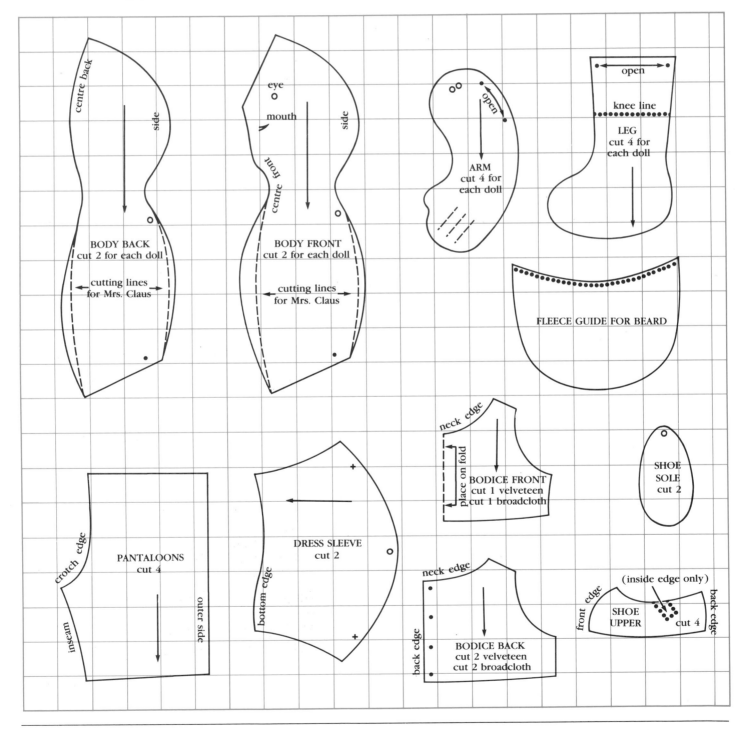

cut body fronts, body backs, arms and legs.

For Mrs. Claus: From flesh-tone broadcloth, cut arms, then following broken pattern lines, cut body fronts and backs. From striped cotton, cut legs.

2. **Legs:** With right sides together, stitch 2 leg pieces together, leaving open at top. Clip curves. Turn right side out. Stuff to dotted line (knee). Fold leg so front and back seams align. Topstitch across knee line. Stuff upper leg lightly and machine-stitch closed 6 mm from raw edge. Repeat for other leg.

3. **Body:** With right sides together, stitch 2 body front pieces down centre front seam and 2 body back pieces down centre back seam. Clip curves. With right sides together and toes pointing toward tummy, stitch legs to bottom edge of body front. With right sides together, stitch body front to body back, leaving bottom edge open between dots. Clip curves. Turn right side out. Stuff head, maintaining shape of nose and chin. Stuff body firmly. Turn under 6 mm around bottom edge. Slipstitch opening closed.

4. **Arms:** With right sides together, stitch 2 arm pieces together, leaving open between dots. Clip curves. Turn right side out. Stuff firmly. Turn under 6 mm around opening. Slipstitch closed. Topstitch finger lines on hand. Repeat for other arm.

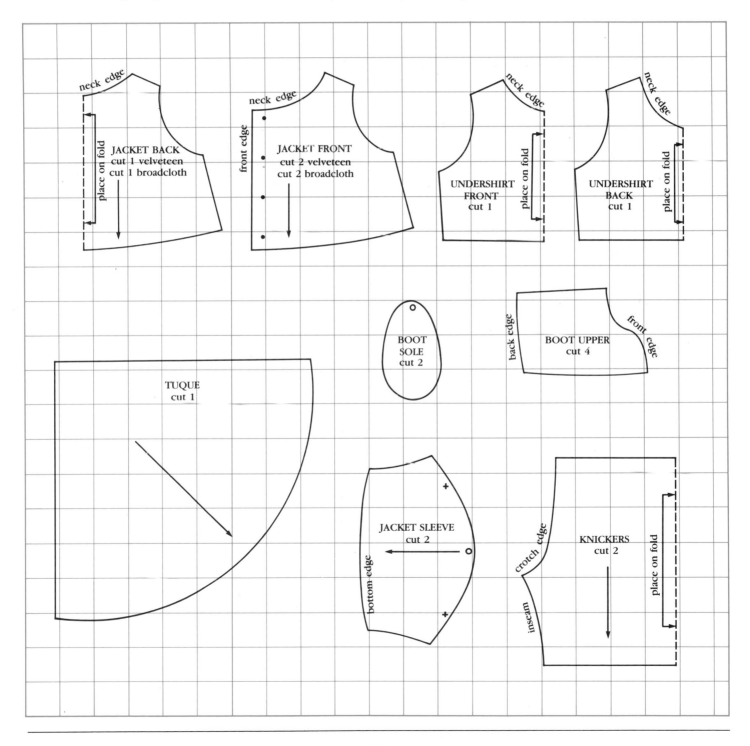

Thread doll-making needle with flesh-tone buttonhole thread. Stitching through shoulder circles, push needle through one arm, through body and out through other arm several times. Thread a clear bead onto last stitch on outside of each arm. Knot thread securely. To allow arm movement, wind buttonhole thread around threads between each arm and shoulder, forming a short shank.

5. **Face:** Mark placement of eyes with pins. Thread doll-making needle with flesh-tone buttonhole thread. Push needle in at top of head and out at one eye. Push needle back into same eye, taking a 3 mm (1/8-in) stitch, and out at other eye. Shape bridge of nose by pinching nose firmly while stitching several times through face from eye to eye, pulling thread tightly. Push needle out at top of head. Knot thread securely. Thread needle with blue buttonhole thread. Push needle in at back of head, out at one eye and through blue button. Push needle back through button and out at back of head, pulling button tightly toward back of head. Repeat 3 or 4 times. Repeat for other eye.

With a single strand of floss and outline stitch, embroider mouth. Color cheeks lightly with colored pencil.

6. **Hair:** Shape a handful of fleece into a circle approx 15 cm (6 in) in diameter and 5 cm (2 in) thick, having long fibres running in same direction. Supporting fleece with both hands, gently dip in several times into lukewarm water. Set fleece on a towel and blow-dry with hair dryer on low setting. As it dries, mold and fluff fleece into shape to fit doll's head. When dry, pin to head so fibres run from side to side. Arrange curls and wisps to frame face and trim off any excess. Tack hair to top of head and around hairline using tiny stitches 2 cm (3/4 in) apart. Stitch a line of closely spaced stitches down centre of head for part. Spray lightly with starch.

7. **Beard and moustache (Santa only):** Prepare fleece as for hair. As it dries, mold and fluff it into the beard shape shown on pattern, having fibres running lengthwise. Along face edge indicated by dotted line, wrap some fibres to underside to give a smooth edge. Tack to chin and cheeks. Fluff out and trim. Spray lightly with starch.

Form moustache from fleece. Pinch in at centre and tack securely in place under nose. Spray lightly with starch.

CLOTHES — MRS. CLAUS

1. **Shoes:** From black felt, cut shoe uppers, shoe soles and 2 straps, 8 cm × 6 mm (3-1/8 × 1/4 in). Edgestitch along 2 long edges and 1 short end of each strap. Stitch front edge of 2 shoe uppers together using a 3 mm (1/8-in) seam allowance. On one side only, pin unstitched end of strap to inside edge of upper where indicated by dotted line. Edgestitch around top edge of upper, catching strap in stitching. With right sides together and using a 3 mm seam allowance, stitch back seam then stitch sole to bottom edge of upper (match circle to centre front seam). Turn right side out. Repeat for other shoe, attaching strap to opposite side so you will have a right and a left shoe.

Slip shoes on doll, having straps at inside of each foot. Cross straps over feet and secure to outside of each shoe with a few hand stitches. Thread a black bead onto last stitch and knot thread securely.

2. **Pantaloons:** Cut pantaloons from polka-dot fabric. With right sides together, stitch 2 pieces together down side seam. Press seam open. Turn under 3 mm then 6 mm along bottom edge. Topstitch. Stitch 20 mm wide gathered lace along hemmed edge. With right sides together stitch inseam. Repeat with remaining 2 pantaloon pieces.

Turn one leg right side out and insert into other leg so right sides are together and inseams are aligned. Stitch crotch seam. Turn pantaloons right side out. Run 2 rows of gathering stitches around top edge. Cut a 26 cm (10-1/4-in) length of 6 mm white elastic. Overlap and stitch ends together. Pin elastic around top edge of pantaloons, adjusting gathers to fit. Machine-zigzag in place. Remove gathering threads.

3. **Petticoat:** From white woven-stripe fabric, cut a 66 × 12 cm (26 × 4-3/4-in) rectangle. Fold in half so right sides are together and short edges meet. Stitch short edges together. Press seam open.

Turn under 3 mm then 6 mm around one raw edge. Topstitch. Stitch right side of 40 mm gathered lace to wrong side of hemmed edge. Gather top edge and attach elastic as for pantaloons.

4. **Dress:** From velveteen, cut bodice front, bodice backs, sleeves and a 66 × 20 cm (26- × 7-7/8-in) rectangle for skirt. From broadcloth, cut bodice front, bodice backs (facings) and 2 bias strips, 14 × 3.5 cm (5-1/2 × 1-3/8 in) for sleeve facings. With right sides together, stitch bodice front to bodice backs at shoulders. Press seams open. Repeat with bodice facings. With right sides of bodice and facing together, stitch down back and around neck edges. Clip curves. Turn right side out. Press. Baste bodice to facing around armholes, waist and side edges.

With right sides together, stitch one long edge of sleeve facing along cuff edge of sleeve. Gather top edge of sleeve between Xs. With right sides together, pin sleeve to armhole, matching circle to shoulder seam and adjusting gathers evenly. Stitch. Remove gathering threads. Trim seam allowance to 3 mm and zigzag along raw edges. Repeat for other sleeve. With right sides together, stitch sleeve and side seams. Turn under 6 mm on raw edge of sleeve facings. Fold facings under along seam line and slipstitch to wrong side.

Gather one long edge of skirt. Press under 13 mm (1/2 in) on each short edge. With right sides together, pin gathered edge of skirt to bodice, aligning folds at each end with back edges of bodice and adjusting gathers evenly in between. Stitch. Open out folded edges of skirt. With right sides together and using a 13 mm seam allowance, stitch centre back seam to within 7 cm (2-3/4 in) of bodice seam. Press seam open. Machine-zigzag raw edges of seam allowance. Machine-zigzag along bottom edge of skirt. Turn under 5 cm (2 in) and hem. Slipstitch 10 mm flat lace over raw edge of hem. Slipstitch 10 mm gathered lace around inside edge of neck and cuffs. Sew 4 snap fasteners to bodice back. On outside of bodice, sew a red bead over each snap.

5. **Apron:** From white woven-check fabric, cut a 30 × 19 cm (11-7/8- ×

7-1/2-in) rectangle for apron, two 9 cm (3-1/2-in) squares for pocket and a 93 × 5 cm (36-5/8- × 2-in) strip for tie. Turn under 3 mm then 6 mm along short edges of apron. Topstitch. Turn under 6 mm then 4 cm (1-5/8 in) along one long edge. Topstitch. Press under 6 mm along one edge of each pocket square. With right sides together and folded edges matching, stitch 2 pocket squares together along three raw edges. Clip corners. Turn right side out. Having open edge at bottom, topstitch pocket to apron front. Place pin at centre of long raw edge of apron. Gather this edge. Pull up

gathering thread so gathered edge measures 13 cm (5-1/8 in) long. Knot threads. Place pin at centre of one long edge of tie. With right sides together and centre pins matching, baste apron to tie, adjusting gathers evenly. Fold tie in half so right sides are together and long edges meet. Stitch along unbasted section of long edges and up short ends. Clip corners. Turn right side out. Press. Turn under 6 mm along centre of tie at back of apron. Topstitch opening closed.

6. **Dust cap:** From white woven-check fabric, cut a 42 × 18 cm (16-1/2- × 7-in) rectangle. Fold in half so right sides are

together and short edges meet. Stitch short edges together leaving 6 mm openings 1 cm (3/8 in) from one raw edge (top) and 6 mm from opposite raw edge (bottom). Press seam open. To make top casing, turn under 1 cm around top edge and topstitch 6 mm from fold. To make bottom casing, turn under 4 cm around bottom edge and topstitch first 2.5 cm (1 in) then 3.5 cm (1-3/8 in) from fold. Turn right side out.
Cut a 20 cm length of red ribbon and thread through top casing. Draw up and tie tightly in a bow. Tack bow in place. Cut a 26 cm length of white 3 mm elastic and thread through bottom casing. Overlap and stitch ends together.

CLOTHES — SANTA

1. **Boots:** From black felt, cut boot uppers and boot soles. Stitch front edge of 2 boot uppers together using a 3 mm seam allowance. Stitch piping around inside top edge so rolled edge extends beyond felt. Stitch black velvet ribbon around outside top edge. With right sides together and using a 3 mm seam allowance, stitch back seam then stitch sole to bottom edge of upper (match circle to centre front seam). Turn right side out. Repeat for other boot.

2. **Undershirt:** From striped knit fabric, cut undershirt front and back. With right sides together, stitch front to back at shoulders and sides. Turn under 6 mm on all raw edges. Machine-zigzag or stretch-stitch in place.

3. **Knickers:** From red velveteen, cut knickers. From red broadcloth, cut a strip 36 × 3.5 cm (14-1/4 × 1-3/8 in) for waistband facing. Fold each knicker leg in half along fold line so right sides are together. Stitch inseam. Press seam open. Machine-zigzag around bottom edge. Run 2 lines of gathering stitches around bottom edge. Cut a 10 cm (4-in) length of 6 mm elastic. Overlap and stitch ends together. Pin elastic around inside bottom edge, adjusting gathers evenly. Machine-zigzag in place. Remove gathering threads. Repeat for other leg. Turn one leg right side out and insert into other leg so right sides are together and inseams are aligned. Stitch crotch seam. Turn knickers right side out. Fold waistband facing in half so right

sides are together and short ends meet. Stitch short ends together. With right sides together, stitch one edge of facing around waist of knickers. Turn under 6 mm or remaining raw edge. Fold facing to inside along seam. Slipstitch in place. Slip knickers on doll.

4. **Suspenders:** Cut two 20 cm lengths of twill tape. Pin one end of each to back waist of knickers, 1 cm to either side of seam. Cross tapes, bring over shoulders and pin ends to front waist, 2 cm (3/4 in) to either side of seam. Stitch red buttons to back of knickers over tape ends. Tack tapes together at crossover and sew on a small diamond of red felt. At front, stitch snap fasteners to tape ends and to waist. Stitch red buttons to outside of suspenders over each snap fastener.

5. **Jacket:** From velveteen, cut jacket back, fronts and sleeves. From broadcloth, cut jacket back and fronts (facings). With right sides together, stitch jacket fronts to back at shoulders. Press seams open. Repeat with facings. With right sides of jacket and facing together, stitch down front and around neck edges. Clip curves. Turn right side out. Press. Baste jacket to facing around armholes, bottom and side edges. From fake fur, cut 2 strips 12 × 3.5 cm for cuff trim and 1 strip 42 × 4 cm for hem trim. From broadcloth, cut the same on the bias, for trim facings.

With right sides together, stitch one long edge of cuff facing to cuff trim. Finger-press seam allowance toward trim and secure with tiny catch stitches. With right sides together, stitch opposite long edge of cuff trim to cuff edge of sleeve. Finger-press as before.

Gather top edge of sleeve between Xs. With right sides together, pin sleeve to armhole, matching circle to shoulder seam and adjusting gathers evenly. Stitch. Remove gathering threads. Trim seam allowance to 3 mm and zigzag along raw edges. Repeat for other sleeve.

With right sides together, stitch sleeve and side seams. Turn under 6 mm on raw edge of cuff facings. Fold facings under along seam line and slipstitch to wrong side.

Stitch hem trim and facing together and sew to bottom edge of jacket as for cuff trim. Turn under 6 mm on raw edge of facing. Fold along seam line so right side of trim and facing are together. Stitch ends in line with front edges of jacket. Clip corners. Turn right side out. Slipstitch facing to wrong side.

Sew 4 snap fasteners down front of jacket. On outside, sew a red bead over each snap.

6. From velveteen, cut tuque. From fake fur, cut a strip 35 × 3.5 cm (13-7/8 × 1-3/8 in) for trim and a 3.5 cm diameter circle for pom-pom. From broadcloth, cut

a bias strip 35 × 3.5 cm, for trim facing. Stitch trim and facing together and sew to curved edge of tuque as for cuff trim. Fold so right sides are together and straight edges meet. Stitch straight edges together. Turn under 6 mm on raw edge of facing. Fold facing under along seam line and slipstitch to wrong side. Run a line of gathering stitches around edge of fur circle. Place a small amount of fibrefill on wrong side. Pull up gathering thread to form a ball. Knot thread. Slipstitch closed. Sew pom-pom to tip of tuque.

7. **Sack:** From velveteen, cut a 32 × 20 cm (12-5/8- × 7-7/8-in) rectangle and a 9 cm (3-1/2-in) diameter circle. Fold rectangle in half so right sides are together and short edges meet. Stitch short edges together, leaving a 1 cm opening 7 cm (2-3/4 in) from one corner (top edge). Machine-zigzag around top edge. Turn under 4 cm. To make casing, topstitch 3.5 cm then 2.5 cm from fold. Run 2 lines of gathering stitches around bottom edge. With right sides together, pin gathered edge around circle, adjusting gathers evenly. Stitch. Remove gathering threads. Machine-zigzag raw edge. Turn right side out.

Cut red cord in half. Thread both lengths through casing. Tie a bell to end of each cord.

HOMESPUN NATIVITY

This simple crèche scene, symbolic of the first Christmas, expresses the true spirit of the season. The figures are dressed in homespun fabrics and assorted trims are added for an effect that is both natural and artistic. It's a heartwarming scene destined to become the focal point of your Christmas celebrations.

DESIGN BY MARY CORCORAN

YOU NEED (*for 8 figures*):
- .40 m linen fabric, 115 cm wide
- 8 pieces of co-ordinating linen fabric, each 18 cm (7 in) square, for cloaks
- 1.40 m ecru lace or ribbon, 10 mm wide
- Assorted scraps of lace trim
- Matching threads

- Polyester fibrefill
- Piece of cardboard, 20.5 cm (8 in) square
- 2 wooden beads, 25 mm in diameter
- Small beads or pebbles
- Large wooden bead and small piece of cork to fit hole in bead
- 3 twigs, approx 18 cm (7 in) long

- White craft glue
- Gesso
- Stiff-bristle artist's paintbrush
- Red and black permanent fine-tip felt markers
- Geometry compass
- Brown paper

Simple yet symbolic, Homespun Nativity is a work of art.

TO MAKE:

To enlarge body pattern, see General Directions (page 134).

Note: Use a 6 mm (1/4-in) seam allowance throughout.

1. From large length of linen, cut 8 bodies, eight 12.5 × 4 cm (5- × 1-5/8-in) rectangles for arms, eight 8.5 cm (3-3/8-in) diameter base circles and three 6.5 × 5 cm (2-1/2- × 2-in) rectangles, one for baby body, one for diaper and one for lamb.

From cardboard, cut eight 5.5 cm (2-1/8-in) diameter base circles and 1 face shape to be used as a pattern only.

2. **Face:** Fold each body in half lengthwise so wrong sides are together. Having fold on left side for 4 figures and on the right side for remaining 4 figures, centre and trace around face pattern 2 cm (3/4 in) below top edge of body. Paint face with gesso. Let dry. Apply 2 more coats. With markers, practice drawing facial features on scrap paper. Select the ones you like best and draw them on the fabric faces.

3. **Hair and beard:** Unravel threads from leftover fabric. For straight hair and beard, wrap strands of thread around hairline and under chin. Tack in place. For curly hair, loop 5 strands of thread as shown in Diagrams 1 and 2 and tack to head and around face. For Mary, gather together several strands of thread and tie in the middle. Tack to centre and down sides of head.

Diagram 1   Diagram 2

4. **Body:** Fold each body so right sides are together. Stitch side seam. With doubled thread, run a line of gathering stitches around top edge. Pull up thread and knot securely. Turn body right side out. Stuff. Turn under 6 mm around bottom edge.

5. **Base:** Run a line of gathering stitches around edge of each fabric base. Place cardboard base inside fabric circle. Pull up thread and gather evenly around cardboard. Knot securely. Slipstitch base to bottom of body.

6. **Arms:** Fold each arm piece in half so right sides are together and long edges meet. Stitch long raw edge and both ends. Cut in half so you have 2 narrow tubes. Clip corners. Turn both tubes right side out. Stuff each arm lightly. Hand-stitch finger lines at closed end, pulling gently on stitches to make hand curve slightly. Slipstitch open end of arms to each side of body.

7. **Cloak:** Topstitch along one edge (bottom) of each cloak square, 6 mm from edge. Fray edge. Topstitch lace along bottom edge just above fringe. Turn under 6 mm on remaining raw edges. Topstitch. Centre top of cloak over head. Pin top corners underneath arms about 2.5 cm (1 in) below face. Pin bottom corners in place in line with top corners. Smooth fabric from hem up to arms. Pin just below arms, making a small fold to form sleeves. Tack edges of sleeves to body. Remove pins. Slipstitch lace trim around heads of wise men.

8. **Baby:** Fold baby fabric in half so right sides are together and long edges meet. Stitch long edge. Run a line of gathering stitches around one end. Pull up thread and knot securely. Turn right side out. Stuff. Turn under 6 mm around open end. Slipstitch closed. Paint a small face on one end of body with 3 coats of gesso. Let dry. Draw features. Slipstitch lace trim around length of baby's body. Slipstitch baby in Mary's arms.

9. **Diaper:** Topstitch around diaper, 6 mm from edge. Fray edges. Fold in half and slipstitch in Joseph's hands.

10. **Lamb:** Fold lamb fabric in half so right sides are together and long edges meet. Stitch long edge and one end, curving stitching at end to form lamb's head. Trim. Turn right side out. Stuff. Turn under 6 mm around open end. Slipstitch closed. Paint both sides of one end of body (head) with gesso. Let dry. Draw eyes and nose. With 3 strands of unravelled linen, make loops for ears and fleece. Tack in place. Slipstitch lamb in shepherd's arms.

11. Slipstitch twigs in hands of each shepherd.

12. Glue small beads or pebbles onto wooden buttons to represent frankincense and myrrh. Glue cork into hole in large beads to represent a vessel of gold. Glue gifts in hands of wise men.

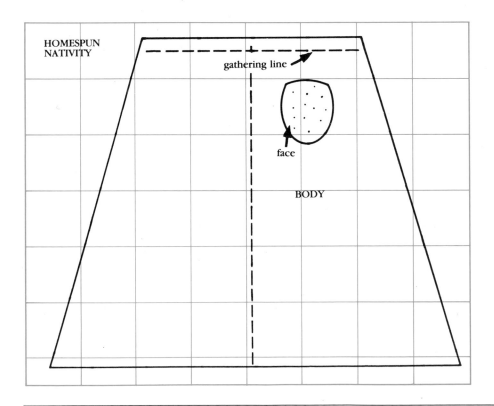

HOMESPUN NATIVITY

gathering line

face

BODY

STAINED GLASS MANGER SCENE

Stained glass is a beautiful medium to interpret the simplicity of the nativity. Even if you've never worked with stained glass, this design is easy enough to assure success.

DESIGN BY RANDY LANCASTER

Finished scene measures 19 × 14 cm (7-1/2 × 5-1/2 in). It is constructed using lead came, but a foiling technique can be used if desired. If foiling, use wire for faces on Mary and shepherd.

YOU NEED:
- **Stained glass in the following colors: white for stable, blue for Mary, red for shepherd, white for sheep and amber for manger**
- **Piece of mirror, approx 20 cm (8 in) square, for base**
- **1 small clear nugget, approx 10 mm in diameter, for baby's head**
- **1 small white nugget, approx 10 mm in diameter, for sheep's head**
- **Approx 46 cm (18 in) copper wire for star, crook, halos and sheep**
- **1 strip each of u lead came in the following sizes: 3/32 in for figures and 9/64 in for stable and base**
- **Wire solder, 60% tin/40% lead solid core (50% tin/50% lead can be used but must be solid core)**
- **Water-soluble flux**
- **Permanent fine-tip marker**
- **Protective goggles or glasses**
- **Glass cutter**
- **Soldering iron**
- **Silicone carbide grinding paper or grinder if available**
- **Utility knife for cutting lead**
- **Pliers**
- **Liquid detergent**
- **Warming candle and holder**
- **Brown paper**

TO MAKE:
To enlarge pattern, see General Directions (page 134).

1. Cut out pattern pieces. Using marker, trace patterns onto corresponding glass.

2. Using glass cutter, cut glass carefully. Using grinding paper or grinder, smooth rough edges. Be sure to wear goggles while grinding.

3. Wrap all figures, manger and nuggets in 3/32-in came. Wrap base and stable pieces in 9/64-in came. Lead stable in 2 parts: first bottom and sides, then roof, extending lead on both sides to create an overhang. Make all joins at a point that will be soldered over when assembling finished unit (e.g. Mary — came should start and finish at bottom back of her gown so join will be hidden when Mary is attached to base). Solder all joins.

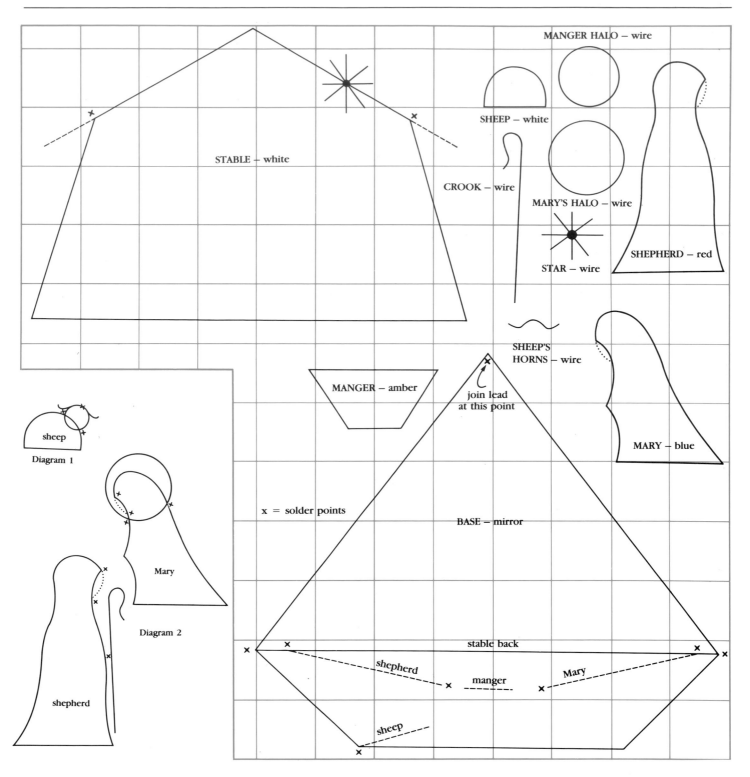

MANGER HALO – wire

SHEEP – white

CROOK – wire

MARY'S HALO – wire

STAR – wire

SHEPHERD – red

STABLE – white

SHEEP'S HORNS – wire

MANGER – amber

join lead at this point

MARY – blue

sheep

Diagram 1

x = solder points

BASE – mirror

Mary

Diagram 2

stable back

shepherd

manger

Mary

shepherd

sheep

4. Bend and cut wire to form star, crook, horns and halos following shapes given on pattern. Flux and tin copper wire before assembling star. Flux and tin horns.

5. Solder white nugget to sheep body at points X (Diagram 1). Solder horns in place.

6. Solder clear nugget to centre top of manger. Solder halo to back of nugget.

7. Using small piece of came, shape a face for shepherd and for Mary as indicated by dotted lines (Diagram 2). Solder in place. Solder halo to back of Mary's head. Solder crook to shepherd.

8. Referring to pattern, solder stable back

in upright position to base across widest section. Solder bottom of figures to came around front of base. Solder star to edge of roof.

9. Clean finished scene by washing in hot soapy water. Rinse well.

10. Place candle in holder. Place behind stable.

CANDLE CAROUSEL

An authentic German carousel was the inspiration for this design. Create a little magic at your workbench and add a bit of old world charm each time you unwrap this heirloom. As the candles flicker and burn, the carolers turn around and around — a fantasy world in miniature.

DESIGN BY HUGH HOPE

The carousel can be made from materials available at any good hardware store, using simple tools. Glue it together or leave it unglued so it can be easily dismantled for storage.

YOU NEED:
• Piece of 3/8-in plywood, 9 × 6 in
• Piece of 1/4-in plywood, 5 × 5 in
• 3/4- × 3/8-in mahogany parting strip or doorstop, 6 ft long
• 1/32- × 3-in sheet balsa wood, 5 ft long
• 1-in lengths of wooden dowel, 1 each in the following diameters: 1/8 in, 3/8 in, 1/2 in, 3/4 in
• 4 wooden doorknobs, each 1-in diameter, for candle holders
• Wooden doorknob, 1-1/2-in diameter
• Wooden doorknob, 2-in diameter
• Circular wooden plate, 3/16 in thick, 2-1/2-in diameter
• 4 round natural-colored wooden beads, 12 mm (1/2-in) diameter
• 4 No. 6 flathead wood screws, 5/8 in long
• Brass-plated flush finger pull, 3/4-in diameter
• 1/16-in rigid wire rod or piano wire, 10 in long
• Contact cement or epoxy glue
• Hacksaw
• Coping saw
• Fine file
• Hammer
• Screwdriver
• Drill with 3/32-in, 1/16-in and 5/16-in bits
• Bolt, with 1/2-in-diameter rounded head, 1 in long
• X-acto knife
• Medium and fine sandpaper
• Carbon paper
• Red and blue paint
• 12 clothespins
• Lemon oil
• 2 cloth rags
• 4 candles, 1/2-in diameter, 3-1/2-in long

TO MAKE:
For full-size pattern pieces, see pages 138 and 139.

Notes: Use carbon paper to transfer outline of pattern pieces onto wood. When cutting notches in base section, uprights and top section, cut slightly smaller than shown in diagrams. Check fit of dovetailed pieces, then sand notches with medium sandpaper until exact fit is obtained.

Label upright pieces and notches A, B, C and D. Fit each piece individually.

Sand all wooden pieces with medium sandpaper until desired size and shape are obtained. Finish with fine sandpaper.

BASE SECTION

1. Cut 12-sided baseplate from 3/8-in plywood. Cut 1/8-in deep notches at A, B, C and D.

2. Drill a 3/32-in hole through centre of baseplate, for wire rod (see Diagram 2).

3. To prepare finger pull to receive pointed end of wire rod, make a slightly rounded indentation by gently hammering roundheaded bolt into bottom of pull.

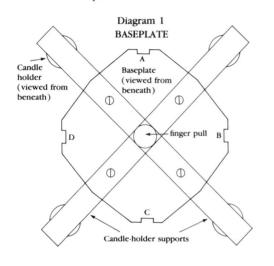

Diagram 1
BASEPLATE

Candle holder (viewed from beneath)

Baseplate (viewed from beneath)

D

finger pull

B

Candle-holder supports

4. Glue finger pull under baseplate, in centre (see Diagrams 2 and 3).

5. From parting strip, cut 4 candle-holder supports, each 4-1/8 in long. Make 1/8- × 3/16-in notches at inside top of each.

6. Position 4 candle-holder supports as shown in Diagram 1, with notches at inside top, securing finger pull in place. Glue in place. Drill holes and secure each support to baseplate with 5/8-in wood screws, as shown in Diagram 2.

7. To make candle holders, drill 5/16-in holes 1/2 in deep in centres of four 1-in wooden doorknobs, as shown in Diagram 2.

8. Glue candle holders in place 1/4 in from outer edge of supports, as shown in Diagram 2.

UPRIGHTS AND TOP SECTION

1. Cut 4 uprights (A, B, C and D) from parting strip.

2. From 3/8-in plywood, using coping saw, cut a circle, 2-1/2 inches in diameter for top plate. Make 1/4-in deep notches at A, B, C and D.

3. Insert lower part of uprights into baseplate notches A, B, C and D; do not glue.

4. Insert top of uprights into top-plate notches A, B, C and D; do not glue. Fit each upright separately, widening notch carefully, until exact fit is obtained.

5. Drill 3/32-in hole through centre of circular wooden plate.

6. Drill 3/32-in hole through centre of 1-1/2-in wooden doorknob.

7. Glue doorknob to plate. Position both on top plate, to form top section (see Diagram 3).

ROTATING CENTRE SECTION

1. Using coping saw, cut a circle 4 in in diameter from 1/4-in plywood. Drill a 1/16-in hole through centre.

2. From 3/4-in dowel, cut a piece 3/4 in long for tree base. Drill a 1/16-in hole lengthwise through centre of dowel.

3. Across top of dowel, make a cut 1/4 in deep and 1/16 in wide. At right angles to first cut, make a cut 1/4 in deep and 1/32 in wide. (See Diagram 3, tree base, top view.)

4. Glue tree base to centre of 4-in circle, as shown in Diagram 3.

5. Using fine file, file one end of wire rod to a very sharp point.

6. Insert rod into tree base and 4-in circle until pointed end projects 1 in. It may be necessary to enlarge hole slightly to allow rod to pass through, but rod should fit *tightly*.

7. Using carbon paper, transfer 3 outlines of tree onto balsa.

8. Using X-acto knife, cut out 2 tree shapes. Insert one into 1/16-in cut in top of tree base. Insert other into same cut, with wire rod sandwiched between the 2 tree shapes. Glue together at outside edges, clamp with clothespins (6 on each side) while glue dries.

9. Cut out third tree shape and cut in half vertically. Insert one half into 1/32-in cut in tree base and glue perpendicular to joined tree shapes. Repeat with other half on other side.

CAROLERS: (*make 2*)

1. From 1-1/2-in length of parting strip, cut body outlines (side view).

2. To make head, file top of 1/2-in bead slightly flat to receive hat.

3. From 1/2-in dowel, cut a piece 1/16 in long, for hat brim.

4. From 3/8-in dowel, cut a piece 1/8 in long, for hat crown.

5. Glue 2 dowel pieces together to make hat. Glue hat to top of head.

6. Glue head to top of body.

7. On face, paint eyes (blue) and mouth (red).

8. Cut several inches of parting strip into 2 pieces 3/16 in wide, for making arms. Cut arms outline (side view). Round edges with sandpaper. File notches at end of arms to receive carol book.

9. Cut carol book from balsa wood. Glue to hands.

DRUMMER:

1. Make body, head and hat as for carolers.

2. From 3/8-in dowel, cut a 1/4-in piece for drum. Glue to front of body.

3. From 3/16-in-wide parting strip, cut arms.

4. From balsa wood, cut 2 pieces 5/8 in long for drumsticks. Glue to hands.

HORN PLAYER:

1. Make body, head and hat as for carolers.

2. Sand one end of 1/8-in piece of dowel to a point for horn.

3. From 3/16-in wide-parting strip, cut arms.

4. Glue arms to body, and horn to arms. Glue figures to centre section around tree, as in photo.

BLADE SECTION

1. Using coping saw, cut a circle 1-1/2 in in diameter from 3/8-in plywood. In bottom of circle, drill a 1/16-in hole 1/4 in deep.

Diagram 2

CANDLE

CANDLE HOLDER

wire rod

BASEPLATE

CANDLE-HOLDER SUPPORT   (cut 4)

sharp point

finger pull

Diagram 3

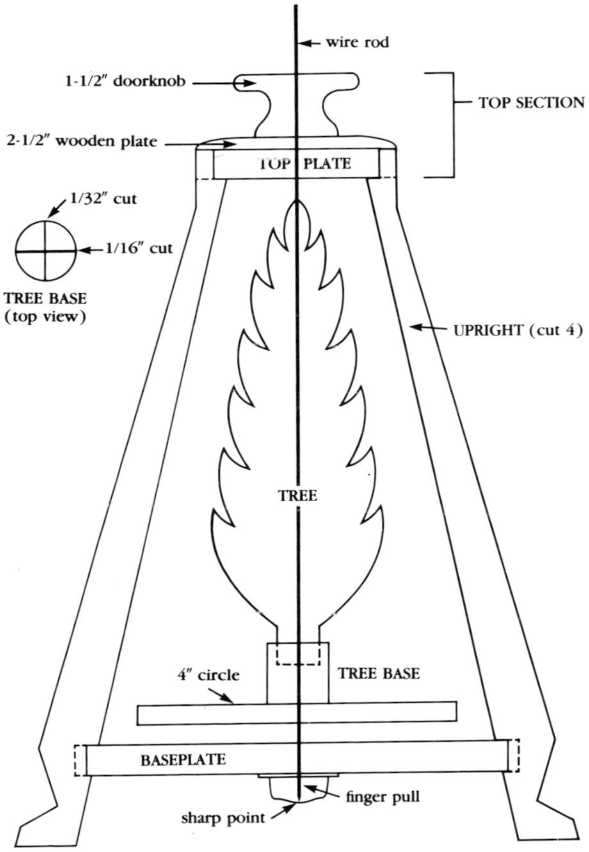

wire rod

1-1/2" doorknob

2-1/2" wooden plate

TOP SECTION

TOP PLATE

1/32" cut

1/16" cut

TREE BASE
(top view)

UPRIGHT (cut 4)

TREE

4" circle

TREE BASE

BASEPLATE

finger pull

sharp point

Diagram 4
BLADE SECTION

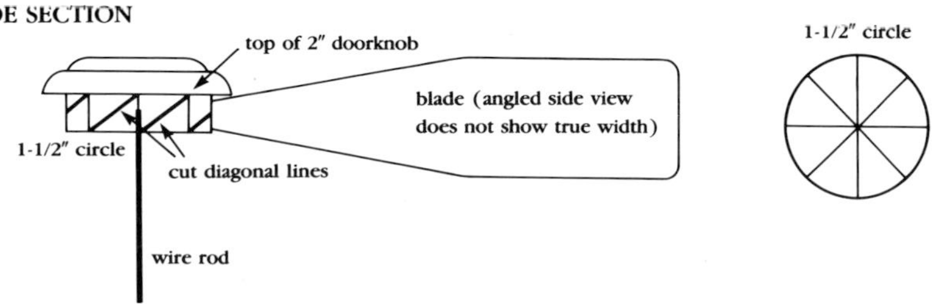

top of 2" doorknob

blade (angled side view does not show true width)

1-1/2" circle

1-1/2" circle

cut diagonal lines

wire rod

2. On both top and bottom of circle, draw lines dividing circle into 8 equal segments, as shown in Diagram 4.

3. Around edge of circle, draw 8 vertical lines connecting top and bottom lines, as shown in Diagram 4.

4. Draw diagonal lines connecting top of one vertical line to bottom of next, as shown in Diagram 4.

5. With hacksaw, cut diagonal lines to depth of 1/4 in.

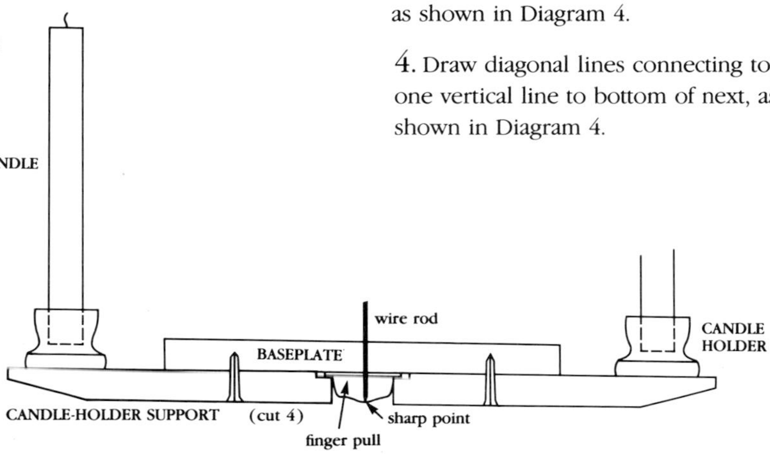

6. From balsa wood, cut 8 blades each 5 × 2-1/2 in. (**Note:** Blade in Diagram 4 is angled and so does not show full width.)

7. Cut top off 2-in doorknob. Glue top to top of 1-1/2-in circle (see Diagram 4).

8. Insert 8 blades into 8 diagonal cuts in 1-1/2-in circle.

TO FINISH:

With rag, rub all wooden pieces with lemon oil. Wipe off excess with dry cloth.

TO ASSEMBLE:

1. Position rotating centre section above base section.

2. Insert pointed end of wire rod into hole of base section. Lower until point rests in indentation in finger pull (see Diagram 3).

3. Insert 4 uprights into base section.

4. Lower top section, inserting top of wire rod through centre hole.

5. Insert tops of 4 uprights into 1/4-in notches in top plate.

6. Position blade section above top section and lower onto top of wire rod. Push down *gently* until blade section is securely fastened to top of wire rod.

7. Base section, uprights and top section can now be glued together or, if desired, left unglued, so that carousel can be dismantled.

TO OPERATE:

1. Ensure that blade and centre section rotates freely.

2. Place candles in candle holders and light. Rotate blades by hand until all 4 candles are lit. To avoid singeing blades, *do not* allow candles to burn when blades are stationary.

3. If blades do not rotate:
a) sharpen point of wire rod further;
b) oil point of wire rod;
c) enlarge holes slightly in base section and top section to ensure centre section moves freely.

STYLIZED NEEDLEPOINT WREATH

*Go beyond the usual Christmas decorations and stitch a festive
wall hanging you'll be proud to display year after year.
This timeless piece of needlepoint is surprisingly
easy to stitch and finish.*

DESIGN BY JOAN PHILLIPS

YOU NEED:

- Piece of white 12-mesh interlock canvas, 46 cm (18-1/8 in) square
- 3-ply Persian yarn, cut into strands 84 cm (33 in) long, in the following colors: 60 strands white, 40 strands medium green, 20 strands bright red and 6 strands dark green
- 19 m gold cloisonné thread for needlepoint
- No. 20 tapestry needle
- Grey Nepo needlepoint marker (waterproof) or water-soluble fabric marker
- Tracing paper
- White paper

For finishing:
- Piece of white cotton, 46 cm square
- Piece of white fabric stiffener, 36 cm (14-1/4 in) square
- Piece of white fusible interfacing, 25 × 12.5 cm (9-7/8 × 5 in)
- White thread
- 37 cm brass rod

TO MAKE:

To enlarge embroidery design on white paper, see General Directions (page 134).

1. Trace embroidery design onto tracing paper and mark centre +. Fold canvas in four to locate centre point. Place canvas over tracing, lining up centre points and lightly outline pattern on canvas using grey marker. Count out and mark a line 15 threads from outer edge of design on all four sides. This marks the inner edge of the first gobelin border row.

2. Using 3 plies (1 full strand) of red yarn (separate the plies before threading needle), embroider the innermost gobelin border, mitring at corners as shown in Diagram 1. In same manner, but with a single strand of cloisonné approx 50 cm (19-3/4 in) long, embroider next gobelin border outside the first, then with 3 plies of medium green, embroider 2 more gobelin borders outside these.

3. Using 2 plies of white yarn and following Diagram 2, fill in background first with horizontal rows then with vertical rows of darning stitches. Make sure you always have enough yarn on needle to complete a row. Watch tension

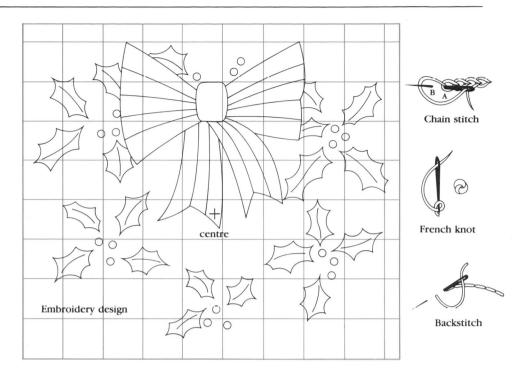

centre

Embroidery design

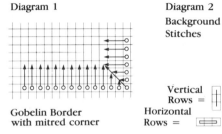

Diagram 1

Gobelin Border with mitred corner

Diagram 2
Background Stitches

Vertical Rows =

Horizontal Rows =

Chain stitch

French knot

Backstitch

*work compensating stitches where necessary

carefully. Where background threads intersect pattern, carry yarn behind canvas under motif area, leaving top surface free for stitching later.

4. Using a single ply of medium green yarn and irregular gobelin stitch to fill space, embroider holly leaves, leaving vein lines free. Using a single ply of dark green yarn and chain stitch, embroider veins. Using a single ply of red yarn and French knots, embroider berries. Using 3 plies of red and 3 plies of white yarn and irregular gobelin stitch, embroider bow and bow tails in alternating red and white stripes (refer to photo). Embroider bow knot in same manner, using a single strand of red yarn. With cloisonné, backstitch between colored stripes on bow and bow tails.

TO BLOCK:

Immerse finished stitchery in tepid water and mild soap. Do not wring. Rinse in clear water. Roll gently in a heavy towel

to remove excess moisture. Pin to a fabric-covered board with pushpins. Let dry thoroughly before removing.

TO FINISH:

1. Trim canvas to within 2.5 cm (1 in) of stitched borders on all sides. Cut fusible interfacing into 4 strips, 25 × 3 cm (9-7/8 × 1-1/8 in). Cut square of fabric stiffener, 6 mm (1/4 in) less than exact size of design. Centre on back of canvas and fuse all four edges in place with strips of fusible interfacing.

2. Fold edges of canvas to back of work, mitring at corners. Hand-stitch in place.

3. Cut cotton for backing, 2.5 cm larger than exact size of design on bottom and sides, 5 cm (2 in) larger at top. Press these allowances under. Topstitch 6 mm then 4.5 cm (1-3/4 in) from top fold to form pocket for hanging rod. Slipstitch backing to back of interfaced stitchery. Insert rod into pocket.

Canadian Living

GLORIOUS CHRISTMAS CRAFTS

CRAFTS FOR BAZAARS

CHAPTER V

BAZAAR BESTS

Nothing makes a bazaar a success more than high-quality, handmade articles. Here are fourteen irresistible ideas that are definite super sellers for any Christmas bazaar or sale. Choose from such great items as tiny Pinecone Teddies, festive Napkin Rings and adorable Pipe-Cleaner Clowns. Most are easy to make in quantity and easy on the budget, too. Included in the collection is a whimsical reindeer — make him your mascot or offer him as a prize in a money-making raffle.

SNOWFLAKE SKI BAND AND MITTS

To fit average-sized woman's head and hand size.

YOU NEED:

- 2 balls (50 g) Patons Canadiana yarn, MC
- 1 ball (40 g) Patons Valencia yard, CC
- 1 ball (50 g) Patons Cotton Sahara yarn, A
- One pair 4.00 mm needles
- 4.00 mm circular needle, 40 cm long OR whichever needles you require to produce the tension given below
- 4.00 mm crochet hook

TENSION:

21 sts and 28 rows = 10 cm (4 ins) in St st. Work to the exact tension with the specified yarn to obtain satisfactory results.
TO SAVE TIME, TAKE TIME TO CHECK TENSION.

TO MAKE:

See General Directions (page 134) for knitting abbreviations.

Note: The contrasting colored motifs are worked by carrying yarn not in use loosely across back of work, but never over more than 3 sts. When it must pass over more than 3 sts, weave it over and under color in use on next st or at centre of sts it passes over. When changing colors, in order to prevent a hole, pass color to be used under and around to right of color just used.

HEADBAND

With MC and circular needle, cast on 100 sts. Join in a round and place a marker on the first st.

Snowflake Ski Bands and Mitts.

Work in St st (k every round), following ski band graph (rep 20 sts of graph 5 times across round) to end of graph.
Next rnd: Purl
Next rnd: Knit. Break MC and CC.
Join A and work in St st until work in A measures 6 mm (1/4 in) less than work in MC and CC. Break A.
Next rnd: Join MC and knit.
Cast off loosely.

TO FINISH:

Fold headband in half so wrong sides are together. With MC, loosely slipstitch cast-on edge to cast-off edge.

MITTS

Right mitt:

**With MC and straight needles, cast on 40 sts. Work 22 rows in (k1 tb1, p1) ribbing, ending with right side facing for next row.

To make thumb gusset:

Beg with a k row, work 8 rows in St st.**
Row 9: K21, inc 1 st in each of next 2 sts, k to end of row.

Rows 10, 12, 14, and 16: Purl.

Row 11: K21, inc 1 st in next st, k2, inc 1 st in next st, k to end of row.

Row 13: K21, inc 1 st in next st, k4, inc 1 st in next st, k to end of row.

Row 15: K21, inc 1 st in next st, k6, inc 1 st in next st, k to end of row.

Row 17: K3, work row 1 of mitt graph, k3, inc 1 st in next st, k8, inc 1 st in next st, k to end of row.

Row 18: P32, work row 2 of mitt graph, p to end of row.

Row 19: K3, work row 3 of graph, k3, inc 1 st in next st, k10, inc 1 st in next st, k to end of row.

Row 20: P34, work row 4 of graph, p to end of row, 52 sts now on needle.

To make thumb:

K3, work row 5 of graph, k17, turn.

Next row: Cast on 1 st, p cast-on st and next 13 sts, turn.

Next row: Cast on 1 st, k cast-on st and next 14 sts.

Continue even in St st on these 15 sts for 6 cm (2-1/4 ins), ending with right side facing for next row.

Next row: K1, (k2tog) to end of row. Break yarn. Thread end through rem sts. Draw up and fasten securely. Sew thumb seam.

To make remainder of mitt:

With right side of work facing, join yarn to last st on right-hand needle. Pick up and k 2 sts at base of thumb. K across sts on left-hand needle.

Next row: P22, working 2 sts picked up at base of thumb together (counts as 1 st), work row 6 of graph, p to end of row. Keeping continuity of graphed motif as established, work even in St st until work from ribbing measures 15 cm (6 ins), ending with right side facing for next row.

To shape top:

Continue work to end of graph *at same time* work as follows:

Row 1: K1, sl 1, k1, psso, k14, k2tog, k2, sl 1, k1, psso, k to last 3 sts, k2tog, k1.

Row 2: Purl.

Row 3: K1, sl 1, k1, psso, k12, k2tog, k2, sl 1, k1, psso, k to last 3 sts, k2tog, k1.

Row 4: Purl.

Row 5: K1, sl 1, k1, psso, k10, k2tog, k2, sl 1, k1, psso, k to last 3 sts, k2tog, k1.

Row 6: Purl.

Continue dec in this manner, having 2 sts less between dec on every alternate row to 16 sts on needle. Cast off purlways. Sew top and side seams.

Left mitt:

Work as for right mitt from **to**

Row 9: K16, inc 1 st in each of next 2 sts, k to end of row.

Rows 10, 12, 14 and 16: Purl.

Row 11: K16, inc 1 st in next st, k2, inc 1st in next st, k to end of row.

HEADBAND GRAPH

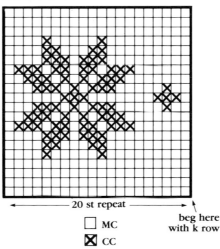

← 20 st repeat →

□ MC
☒ CC

beg here with k row

MITT GRAPH

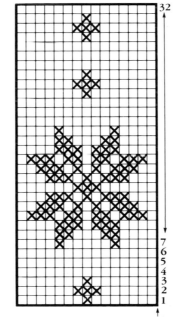

beg here with k row

Row 13: K16, inc 1 st in next st, k4, inc 1 st in next st, k to end of row.

Row 15: K16, inc 1 st in next st, k6, inc 1 st in next st, k to end of row.

Row 17: K16, inc 1 st in next st, k8, inc 1 st in next st, k5, work row 1 of mitt graph, k to end of row.

Row 18: P3, work row 2 of mitt graph, p to end of row.

Row 19: K16, inc 1 st in next st, k10, inc 1 st in next st, k5, work row 3 of mitt graph, k to end of row.

Row 20: P3, work row 4 of mitt graph, p to end of row. 52 sts now on needle.

To make thumb:

K30, turn.

Next row: Cast on 1 st, p cast-on st and next 13 sts, turn.

Next row: Cast on 1 st, k cast-on st and next 14 sts, turn.

Complete thumb as for right mitt.

To make remainder of mitt:

With right side of work facing join, yarn to last st on right-hand needle.

Next row: Pick up and k 2 sts at base of thumb, k4, work row 6 of mitt graph, k to end of row.

Next row: P3, work row 7 of graph, p to end of row, working 2 sts picked up at base of thumb together.

Complete remainder of mitt as for right mitt.

TO FINISH:

With crochet hook, make a chain 183 cm (72 ins) long. Sew ends of chain to mitts.

KNITTED POCKET PEOPLE

The basic method for knitting these dolls is simple. Beginning at feet, knit a rectangle, shaping at top for the head. When body is sewn together and stuffed, arms and legs are defined by stitching through all layers.

YOU NEED:

• **Small quantities of Sayelle or similar-weight yarn in a variety of colors including flesh tone**
• **One pair 3.00 mm needles**
• **3.00 mm crochet hook**
• **Tapestry needle**
• **Embroidery floss**
• **Polyester fibrefill**

TO MAKE:

See General Directions (page 134) for knitting abbreviations.

Note: Work pants in stripes, changing

color every second row and work pullover in solid color St st or vice versa. Cast on 32 sts.

Knit one row, purl one row in same color for feet.

K 24 rows for pants.

Next row (beg hands row): K9 for pants, k3 in flesh tone, k8 for pants, k3 in flesh tone, k9 for pants.

Next row: K8 for pants, p4 in flesh tone, k8 for pants, p4 in flesh tone, k8 for pants.

Next row: K8 for pullover, k4 in flesh tone, k8 for pullover, k4 in flesh tone, k8 for pullover.

Next row: P8 for pullover, p4 in flesh tone, p8 for pullover, p4 in flesh tone, p8 for pullover.

Continue working 14 rows in St st for pullover.

Change to flesh tone and work 15 rows in St st for head as follows:

Rows 1 to 8: Work even in St st.

Row 9: Dec 5 sts evenly across row. 27 sts now on needle.

Row 10: Purl.

Row 11: Dec 5 sts evenly across row. 22 sts now on needle.

Row 12: Purl.

Row 13: Dec 5 sts evenly across row.

17 sts now on needle.

Row 14: Purl.

Row 15: K1, (K2tog) 8 times. Draw yarn through rem sts and pull up.

TO FINISH:

1. Sew sides together to form centre back seam.

2. Stuff head. Weave a single strand of matching yarn through first head row. Draw up to form neck and tie tightly.

3. Stuff body and sew bottom opening closed.

4. With matching yarn, define arms by sewing small backstitches through all layers from waist to 3 rows below neckline. Define legs in the same manner from bottom edge to just below waistline.

5. For hair, cut 10 cm (4-in) lengths of yarn. Attach hair to head as follows: With 2 strands together, fold in half to form a loop. Insert crochet hook into stitch on head, pull hair loop through stitch, then pull yarn ends through loop. Fluff out hair and trim as desired.

6. Using 3 strands of floss, embroider eyes and mouth on face.

Pinecone Teddy.

PINECONE TEDDIES

Design by Mary Corcoran

YOU NEED:

For small bear:
- 4 spruce or balsam cones
- 2 mugho or red pinecones
- 2 leaves cut from white pinecone
- 20.5 cm red ribbon, 6 mm wide
- 30.5 cm red thread
- Glue gun and glue
- Pruning shears

For tiny bear:
- 4 tamarack or balsam cones
- 2 spruce cones
- 2 leaves cut from white pinecone
- 15 cm red ribbon, 3 mm wide
- 23 cm red thread

TO MAKE:

1. Select largest cone for body, medium cone for head and small cones for arms and legs. Lay on table. With base of cones at back, fit leaves of head cone into body cone. Glue together, holding in place until set.

2. Cones for arms and legs can be cut smaller if desired. Glue in place.

3. Fit 2 white pinecone leaves in between leaves of head for ears. Glue in place.

4. To hang, fold thread in half. Knot ends. Loop around bear's neck.

5. Tie a ribbon bow. Glue at front neck. Trim ends.

Make them wild and woolly.
Instructions for Knitted Pocket People begin on p. 89.

PIPE-CLEANER CLOWN

YOU NEED:

- **Bright colored calico, one piece 30 × 20 cm (11-7/8 × 7-7/8 in) and a strip 18 × 3 cm (7 × 1-1/4 in)**
- **Circle of white fine-knit fabric, 6 cm (2-3/8 in) in diameter**
- **.25 m white lace, 20 mm wide**
- **.10 m satin ribbon, 6 mm wide**
- **3 pipe cleaners, each 15 cm (6 in) long**
- **Cotton ball**
- **Small scraps of red and black felt**
- **Small amount of Sayelle yarn for hair**
- **Matching thread**
- **Black thread**
- **White craft glue**
- **Brown paper**

TO MAKE:

To enlarge pattern, see General Directions (page 134).

1. **Body:** Twist 2 pipe cleaners together at one end for 13 mm (1/2 in), then make

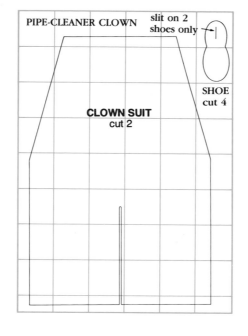

one twist at centre point. Spread untwisted ends apart for legs and bend top section out in shape of a circle for body.

2. **Head:** Run a gathering thread around outer edge of knit fabric circle. Place

cotton ball and top of pipe-cleaner body in centre of fabric and pull up thread so cotton ball and end of pipe cleaners are completely enclosed. Secure thread ends. Using black thread, stitch a cross for each eye. Cut out and glue on a 6 mm (1/4-in) circle of red felt for nose. Using yarn, stitch hair by taking small loops over top and back of head.

3. **Suit:** Cut 2 clown suit pieces from large piece of calico. With right sides together and using a 6 mm seam allowance, stitch up sides and around crotch. Press. Turn right side out. Press under 13 mm at neck and ankle edges. Slip onto pipe-cleaner body. Run a gathering thread around neck edge of suit and draw up tightly. Secure thread ends. Gather ankle edges around legs in same manner, allowing legs to extend 13 mm beyond fabric for feet. Run a gathering thread around one edge of lace to form neck ruffle. Stitch securely in place around neck.

4. **Shoes:** Cut 4 shoes from black felt. Cut a small slit in 2 shoes as indicated on

Amusing Pipe-Cleaner Clowns in bright calico costumes.

pattern. Glue 1 shoe with slit to 1 shoe without slit, inserting pipe-cleaner foot in slit so it is sandwiched between two layers. Repeat for other shoe and foot.

5. Arms: Press under 13 mm at short ends of calico strip. Fold strip in half so right sides are together and long edges meet. Stitch long edges together using a 6 mm seam allowance. Turn right side out. Insert remaining pipe cleaner through this tube, gathering up fabric so pipe cleaner arm extends 13 mm beyond fabric at each end for hands. Slipstitch in place across back of clown just below neck ruffle.

6. Attach ribbon bow and hanging thread to top of head. Bend body in desired pose.

SNOWMAN, DUCK, ANGEL AND SANTA

Designs by Renée Schwarz

Finished ornaments are 8 to 9 cm (3-1/4 to 3-1/2 in) high.
For full-size pattern pieces, see pages 141 and 142.
Note: Use a 6 mm (1/4-in) seam allowance throughout unless otherwise indicated. Backstitch at beginning and end of all seams. Sew fabric *with right sides together*, unless otherwise indicated.

SNOWMAN

YOU NEED:
• **Piece of white sweat suit fleece, 28 ×**

14 cm (11 × 5-1/2 in), for body, head and arms
• **Piece of blue sweat suit fleece, 15 × 9 cm (6 × 3-1/2 in), for hat**
• **Scrap of orange cotton fabric, for nose**
• **Black embroidery floss**
• **Matching thread**
• **Invisible nylon thread**
• **Polyester fibrefill**
• **Small twig**
• **Brown paper**

TO MAKE:

1. Head: From white fleece, cut 2 head sides and 1 head back. Sew 2 side pieces together, leaving open at bottom as indicated. Open up and pin to head back, matching points A. Stitch, leaving a 2.5 cm (1-in) opening at bottom as indicated. Turn right side out. Stuff firmly. Slipstitch opening closed.

2. Body: From white fleece, cut 2 body sides and 1 body bottom. Stitch and stuff as for head. With floss, embroider 3 buttons down centre front seam, 6 mm (1/4 in) apart.

3. Nose: Cut nose from orange fabric. Fold in half lengthwise so right sides are together. Stitch from A to B. Turn right side out. Stuff.

4. Face: Using 2 strands of floss, embroider eyes (satin stitch) on either side of centre front head seam, outlining each with backstitch. Turn under 3 mm (1/8 in) at open end of nose and slipstitch in place on face. With single strand of

floss, embroider small Xs for mouth. Hand-stitch head securely to top of body.

5. Arms: From white fleece, cut 4 arms. Stitch 2 arms together, leaving open at straight end. Turn right side out. Stuff. Make second arm in same manner. Turn under 6 mm at open end of each arm and slipstitch securely to sides of body, approx 2 cm (3/4 in) from buttons.

6. Hat: Cut hat from blue fleece. Fold in half as indicated and stitch, leaving open at bottom. Turn right side out. Turn under 6 mm around open edge and slipstitch in place on head. Fold tip of hat down and tack.

7. Sew twig to 1 arm with invisible thread. Thread hanging loop of invisible thread through top of hat.

DUCK

YOU NEED:
• **Piece of yellow sweat suit fleece, 34 × 14 cm (13-1/2 × 5-1/2 in), for body, head, wings, and tail**
• **Piece of red sweat suit fleece, 15 × 9 cm (6 × 3-1/2 in), for hat and beak**
• **Navy embroidery floss**
• **Matching thread**
• **Invisible nylon thread**
• **Scrap of blue crochet cotton or fine yarn**
• **Crochet hook**
• **Polyester fibrefill**
• **Brown paper**

TO MAKE:

1. Head: Cut pieces from yellow fleece and assemble as for Snowman, Step 1.

2. Body: Cut pieces from yellow fleece and assemble as for Snowman, Step 2.

3. Beak: Cut 2 beaks from red fleece. Stitch together using a 3 mm (1/8-in) seam allowance and leaving open at straight end. Turn right side out. Turn under 3 mm at open end.

4. Face: Using 2 strands of floss, embroider eyes (satin stitch) 3 cm (1-1/4 in) down from top of head on either side of centre front seam, outlining each with backstitch. Slipstitch beak in place just below eyes. Hand-stitch head securely to top of body.

Jolly Snowmen.

Cute little Ducks bundled up in colorful scarves and tuques.

5. Wings: From yellow fleece, cut 4 wings. Stitch 2 wings together, leaving open at straight end. Turn right side out. Stuff. Make second wing in same manner. Turn under 6 mm at open end of each wing and slipstitch securely to sides of body.

6. Tail: Cut 2 tails from yellow fleece. Assemble as for wing and slipstitch to back of body approx 2 cm (3/4 in) from bottom.

7. Hat: Cut piece from red fleece and assemble as for Snowman, Step 6.

8. Crochet a scarf approx 1 cm (3/8 in) wide and 15 cm (6 in) long. Attach a fringe to both ends of scarf. Tie around bird's neck. Thread hanging loop of invisible thread through top of hat.

ANGEL

YOU NEED:
- **Piece of white sweat suit fleece, 16 × 14 cm (6-1/4 × 5-1/2 in), for body and arms**
- **Piece of beige sweat suit fleece, 16 × 10 cm (6-1/4 × 4 in), for head and hands**
- **Piece of heavy fabric stiffener, 9 × 7 cm (3-1/2 × 2-3/4 in)**
- **Piece of white eyelet, 17 × 7 cm (6-3/4 × 2-3/4 in), for wings**
- **Navy, brown and red embroidery floss**
- **Matching thread**
- **Invisible nylon thread**
- **.25 m white lace, 11 mm wide**
- **Scraps of yellow bouclé yarn, for hair**
- **14 cm silver cord, for halo**

- **Polyester fibrefill**
- **Brown paper**

TO MAKE:

1. Head: Cut pieces from beige fleece and assemble as for Snowman, Step 1.

2. Body: Cut angel body and body bottom from white fleece. Fold body in half and stitch straight edges together from A to B. Open up at wide end and stitch to body bottom. Turn right side out. Stuff firmly.

3. Face and trim: Using 2 strands of navy floss, embroider eyes (satin stitch) 3 cm (1-1/4 in) down from top of head on either side of centre front seam, outlining each with backstitch. With single strand of brown floss, embroider a small circle for nose just below eyes. With a single strand of red floss, embroider mouth using backstitch. Turn under 6 mm (1/4 in) at open end of body and hand-stitch head securely to top of body. Hand-stitch lace around neck and bottom of body. Wind bouclé yarn around head for hair and tack in place with matching thread. Bend silver cord into a circle and stitch to back of head to form halo.

Charming cheeky Angels to sell at a bazaar or keep for yourself.

4. Wings: Cut 4 wings from eyelet and 2 from fabric stiffener. Place stiffener between 2 eyelet pieces and satin-stitch around outer edge.
Repeat for second wing. Slipstitch wings to back of body, 6 mm from centre back seam.

5. Thread hanging loop of invisible thread through top of head.

SANTA

YOU NEED:
- **Piece of red sweat suit fleece, 40 × 10 cm (15-3/4 × 4 in), for body, arms and hat**
- **Piece of beige sweat suit fleece, 18 × 7 cm (7 × 2-3/4 in), for head**
- **Scrap of blue sweat suit fleece, for hands**
- **Scrap of yellow cotton fabric, for buckle**
- **17 cm blue bias tape**
- **Black and red embroidery floss**
- **Matching thread**
- **Invisible nylon thread**
- **Scraps of off-white bouclé yarn, for hair and beard**
- **Polyester fibrefill**
- **Brown paper**

TO MAKE:

1. Head: Cut pieces from beige fleece and assemble as for Snowman, Step 1.

2. Body: Cut pieces from red fleece and

assemble as for Snowman, Step 2. With black floss, embroider 2 buttons down centre front seam. Hand-stitch bias tape around body for belt, just below buttons. Cut belt buckle from yellow fabric. Turn under 6 mm (1/4 in) on all edges and hand-stitch in place on belt just under buttons.

3. Face: Using 2 strands of floss, embroider eyes (satin stitch) 3 cm (1-1/4 in) down from top of head on either side of centre front seam, outlining each with backstitch. Embroider red nose just below eyes in same manner. With a single strand of red floss, embroider mouth using backstitch. Hand-stitch head securely to top of body. Wrap bouclé yarn around face for hair and beard and tack in place with matching thread.

4. Arms: From red fleece cut 2 arms and from blue fleece cut 2 hands. Stitch hand to arm. Fold in half so long edges meet and right sides are together. Stitch, leaving open at straight end. Turn right side out. Stuff. Make second arm in same manner. Turn under 6 mm at open end of each arm and slipstitch securely to sides of body.

5. Hat: Cut piece from red fleece and assemble as for Snowman, Step 6.

6. Thread hanging loop of invisible thread through top of hat.

These adorable Santas are bound to be super sellers.

GLITZEN, THE SOCK REINDEER

YOU NEED:
- **Man's work sock, with contrasting color heel and toe**
- **.40 m red calico, 115 cm wide**
- **.25 m each of 5 different printed and plain green cotton fabrics, 115 cm wide, for holly leaves**
- **Piece of green cotton or broadcloth, approx 45 × 35 cm (17-3/4 × 11-3/4 in), for back piece**
- **2 m gold braid, edged with red, 16 mm wide**
- **1 m green satin ribbon, 22 mm wide**
- **1 m green satin ribbon, 12 mm wide**
- **Small scraps of red and black felt**
- **2 gold buttons, 13 mm in diameter**
- **Pair of plastic eyelashes (available at craft supply stores)**
- **Red pom-pom, 16 mm in diameter**
- **Polyester fibrefill**
- **Fabric glue (optional)**
- **Matching thread**
- **Heavy thread**
- **Brown paper**

TO MAKE:
To enlarge pattern, see General Directions (page 134).
Note: Use a 6 mm (1/4-in) seam allowance throughout, unless otherwise indicated. When sewing antler, leaf and back pieces together, use a closely spaced machine stitch.

1. Turn sock inside out. Measure sock length from heel to toe. If longer than 23 cm (9 in), machine-stitch a tuck around sock, approx 18 cm (7 in) from toe, to make correct length. Turn sock right side out. Stuff firmly with fibrefill to within 8 cm (3-1/8 in) of opening. With heavy thread, tie opening tightly closed. Wrap wide green ribbon around closing and tie in a large bow at front.

2. Harness: Pin a length of gold braid around nose, covering tuck seam, so that ends overlap 1.5 cm (5/8 in). Turn under 6 mm along top overlap. Slipstitch braid in place.
Reins: Cut remaining gold braid in half. Turn under 6 mm along one end of each piece. Pin each folded end to

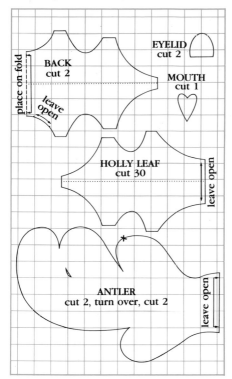

EYELID
cut 2

BACK
cut 2

place on fold

leave open

MOUTH
cut 1

HOLLY LEAF
cut 30

leave open

ANTLER
cut 2, turn over, cut 2

leave open

*Make Glitzen, The Sock Reindeer,
the star attraction at your bazaar.*

harness at each side of head. Pin each rein straight back along side of head and around to centre back, aligning top edge of braid with edge of contrasting color heel. Slipstitch in place. Reinforce stitching at centre back where 2 reins meet. To make hanging loop, tie loose ends of reins in a bow approx 35 cm (13-7/8 in) from join at centre back.

3. **Face:** From red felt, cut heart for mouth. Stitch or glue in place on end of nose. Centre pom-pom above mouth. Stitch or glue in place. With heavy thread,

stitch button eyes and lashes in place. From black felt, cut 2 eyelids. Fit eyelids over lashes, cupping slightly. Stitch or glue in place.

4. **Antlers:** From red calico, cut 4 antlers. With right sides of 2 pieces together, stitch, leaving bottom edges open. Carefully trim seam allowances to 3 mm (1/8 in). Turn right side out. Stuff firmly. Turn under 6 mm around openings. Using heavy thread, stitch antlers to top of head. Tack antlers together at X. Cut narrow green ribbon in half. Wrap 1

length of ribbon around base of each antler. Tie in a bow.

5. **Leaves:** From green cotton, cut 30 holly leaves (6 from each .25 m length of fabric). With right sides of 2 pieces together, stitch, leaving bottom edge open. Carefully trim seam allowance to 3 mm. Turn right side out. Stuff lightly. Turn under 6 mm around opening. Edgestitch opening closed. Machine-quilt centre line of leaf indicated by dotted line. Make 14 more leaves in same manner.

6. **Back:** From green cotton, cut 2 back pieces. With right sides together, stitch, leaving open between notches on one half. Carefully trim seam allowance to 3 mm. Turn right side out. Stuff lightly. Turn under 3 mm around opening. Slipstitch opening closed. Machine-quilt centre line indicated by dotted line.

7. Arrange holly leaves on back, having bottom straight edges toward centre. Hand-stitch in place. Centre reindeer head on top of leaves. Using heavy thread, hand-stitch in place. Tack antlers to leaves, if necessary.

CUDDLY TEDDY

Design by Mary Corcoran

YOU NEED:

- **Pieces of fake fur, 20.5 × 18 cm (8 × 7 in) for body and 35.5 × 10 cm (14 × 4 in) for arms, legs and ears**
- **Red felt, 35.5 × 2 cm (14 × 3/4 in)**
- **2 snap-on glass eyes, 10.5 mm in diameter**
- **2 red pom-poms, 16 mm in diameter**
- **1 red pipe cleaner**
- **Matching thread**
- **Red and dark brown embroidery floss or pearl cotton**
- **Embroidery needle**
- **Polyester fibrefill**
- **Sharp scissors**
- **Dressmaker's chalk**
- **Knitting needle**
- **Glue gun and glue**
- **Brown paper**

TO MAKE:

To enlarge pattern, see General Directions (page 134).

Note: Stitch seams first, then cut, leaving a 6 mm (1/4-in) seam allowance. Backstitch at beginning and end of seams.

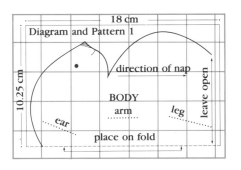

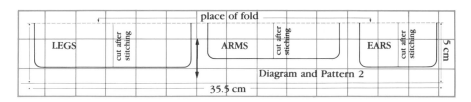

1. Fold body fabric in half so right sides are together and short edges meet. Pin at corners. Lay pattern on fold (see Diagram 1). Using dressmaker's chalk, trace outline and placement markings. *Do not cut out.*

2. With point of scissors, make 2 small eyeholes in face. Insert eye shanks. Push on metal backings on wrong side.

3. With right sides together, fold fabric for arms, legs and ears in half so long edges meet. Pin at corners. Lay pattern pieces along fold (see Diagram 2), leaving a 6 mm seam allowance around each piece. Trace outline and markings. *Do not cut out.*

4. Stitch along all drawn outlines, being sure to leave base of body open. Cut out each piece leaving 6 mm allowance outside stitching lines. Cut ears, arm and leg pieces in half along lines indicated. Clip corners. Turn all pieces right side out.

5. Stuff body firmly using knitting needle to push in small bits of fibrefill. Stuff legs and arms firmly at ends and less firmly toward opening.

6. Using doubled thread, slipstitch open end of ears in place at sides of head. Slipstitch arms and legs to body in the same manner. Slipstitch opening at base of bear closed.

7. Using embroidery floss and satin stitch, embroider brown nose and red mouth.

8. For earmuffs, cut an 8.5 cm (3-1/4-in) length of pipe cleaner. Glue pom-poms to each end of pipe cleaner then glue ends to either side of head in front of ears.

9. For scarf, cut a fringe at each end of felt strip. Tie around neck of bear.

CANDY-CANE CLOWN

Design by Renée Schwarz

The finished clown is approx 37 cm (14-1/2 in) tall.

YOU NEED:

- .15 m red-and-white-striped fabric, 115 cm wide
- Piece of flesh-tone broadcloth, 28 × 19 cm (11 × 7-1/2 in)
- Piece of red broadcloth, 54 × 11 cm (21-1/4 × 4-1/4 in)
- Small scrap of yellow fabric
- .45 m narrow red rickrack
- Navy, red and yellow embroidery floss
- 3 cm (1-1/8 in) white elastic, 6 mm wide

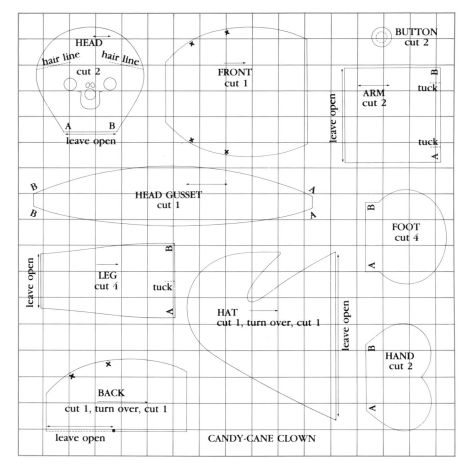

- Green crochet cotton yarn
- Matching thread
- Polyester fibrefill
- Brown paper

TO MAKE:

To enlarge pattern, see General Directions (page 134).

Note: Use a 6 mm (1/4-in) seam allowance unless otherwise indicated. Backstitch at beginning and end of all seams.

1. **Head:** Cut head gusset and 2 head pieces from flesh-tone broadcloth. Trace facial markings onto 1 head piece only. With right sides together, stitch 1 side of gusset to 1 head piece then other side of gusset to second head piece. Turn right side out. Stuff firmly.

Using 2 strands of floss, embroider (satin stitch) navy eyes, red nose, yellow cheeks and red mouth, outlining each with backstitch.

2. From striped fabric, cut 4 legs, 2 arms, 1 front, 2 backs and 2 hats, being sure to flip pattern pieces where indicated. From red cotton, cut 2 hands and 4 feet.

Arms: With right sides together, pin hand to arm from A to B, taking 2 small tucks in arm about 1.5 cm (5/8 in) from each edge to fit. Stitch. Fold arm/hand in half lengthwise so right sides are together. Stitch around hand with red thread and up arm with white thread, leaving top open. Clip curves. Turn right side out. Stuff hand firmly and arm slightly less firmly. Make second arm/hand in same manner.

3. **Legs:** With right sides together, pin foot to leg from A to B, taking a small tuck at centre of leg to fit. Stitch. Repeat with other 3 foot and leg pieces. With right sides of 2 foot/legs together, stitch around foot with red thread and up leg with white thread, leaving top open. Clip curves. Turn right side out. Stuff foot firmly and leg slightly less firmly. Make second foot/leg in same manner.

4. **Body:** With right sides of backs together, stitch from bottom edge to small dot. Pin front to back, placing top

of arms between front and back between Xs so underarm seam faces down. Allow top of arm to project 1 cm (3/8 in) past edge of body. Stitch side seams, reinforcing with a second row of stitching over arms. Turn body right side out. Turn under 1 cm around opening at bottom of body. Insert top of legs. Topstitch in place twice.

Turn under 6 mm (1/4 in) around neck edge. Sew rickrack around neck edge. Pin neck to head and slipstitch securely in place. Stuff body. Turn under 6 mm on back opening edge. Fold elastic in half to form a loop and sew at top of back opening. Clown may be suspended from this hanging loop. Slipstitch back opening closed.

5. **Hair:** Wrap green yarn around a 15 × 2.5 cm (6- × 1-in) strip of paper. Stitch 6 mm from 1 long edge. Cut loops along opposite long edge. Tear away paper and cut fringe in half. Hand-stitch in place on either side of head along broken line indicated on pattern.

6. **Hat:** With right sides of hat together, stitch around curved edge, leaving open at bottom. Clip curves. Turn right side out. Turn under 6 mm around bottom edge. Sew rickrack around bottom edge. Slipstitch securely to head.

7. Cut 2 small circles from yellow fabric for buttons. Turn under edge of each to form a 1 cm circle. Sew circles to front of clown using tiny hand stitches.

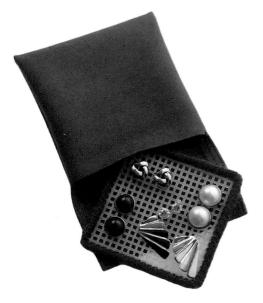

Pierced-Earring Pouch.

PINECONE ORNAMENT

YOU NEED:
- **Pinecone approx 7.5 cm (3 in) long**
- **18 cm florist ribbon, 13 mm wide**
- **Small decorations such as artificial greenery and fruit**
- **Glue gun or white craft glue**
- **Spray varnish**

TO MAKE:
Varnish pinecone. Allow to dry thoroughly. Overlap and glue ends of ribbon together to form a loop. Glue loop to top of pinecone. Glue greenery and decorations in place inside ribbon loop at top of pinecone.

PIERCED-EARRING POUCH

YOU NEED:
- **7.5 cm (3-in) square of plastic needlepoint canvas**
- **Piece of synthetic suede, 26 × 11 cm (10-1/4 × 4-1/4 in)**
- **Small amount of tapestry or Persian yarn to match suede**
- **Matching thread**
- **Small Velcro dot fastener**
- **Velcro glue**

TO MAKE:

1. Bind edges of plastic canvas with tapestry yarn using binding or overcast stitch.

2. Fold one short end of suede up 9.5 cm (3-3/4 in) so right sides are together. Stitch side seams using a 6 mm (1/4-in) seam allowance. Clip corners. Turn right side out.

3. Turn under 6 mm on all edges of flap. Topstitch close to fold then 3 mm (1/8 in) inside this line.

4. Glue Velcro dot in place on flap and on front of caddy.

Pinecone Ornament (top left) and festive Napkin Rings (below).

NAPKIN RINGS

YOU NEED: (for each ring)
- **Wooden curtain ring, 5 cm (2 in) in diameter**
- **Small ribbon bow**
- **Small decorations such as miniature pinecones, artificial greenery or fruit**
- **Glue gun or white craft glue**

TO MAKE:
Glue bow and decorations to ring, covering metal eyelet.

SPRITELY ELF

A beaming little red, white and green elf will help make any bazaar a resounding success. Sew several of them and see how their happy faces and jingle bells turn on the holiday smiles.

DESIGN BY CHRISTINE McCORMACK

YOU NEED:

- .20 m green felt, 180 cm wide
- .40 m red-and-white-striped fabric, 115 cm wide
- Piece of white flannelette, 40 × 30 cm (15-3/4 × 11-7/8 in)
- Scraps of white, red, green and black felt
- Matching threads
- Shank button, 10 mm in diameter
- 3 jingle bells
- Polyester fibrefill
- Brown paper

TO MAKE:

To enlarge pattern, see General Directions (page 134).

Note: Use a 6 mm (1/4-in) seam allowance throughout.

1. Cut body/legs from green felt, head from flannelette and arms and hat from striped fabric. Cut eyes, ears, cheeks, holly leaves and berries from color of felt indicated on pattern.

2. **Body/legs:** Stitch 2 body/legs pieces together from A, around one leg to B, then around other leg to C. Leave open at end. Trim seam allowance. Cut along slash line between legs. Turn right side out. Stuff, using a chopstick to poke fibrefill into legs. Stuff slightly less around fold areas. Turn under 6 mm at open end. Slipstitch closed. Sew bell to tip of each foot.

3. **Arms:** With right sides folded together, stitch raw edge of arms together, leaving a 5 cm (2-in) opening at centre of long edge. Trim seam allowance. Turn right side out. Stuff. Slipstitch opening closed.

4. **Hat:** With right sides together, stitch hat pieces together along long edges. Turn right side out. Turn under 6 mm on bottom edge. Hem. Stitch bell to tip of hat.

5. **Head:** With right sides together, stitch 2 head pieces together on one edge. Open out. With right sides together, stitch third piece to the first 2 pieces, leaving a 5 cm opening in one seam. Trim seam allowances. Turn right side out. Stuff firmly to form round head. Slipstitch opening closed.

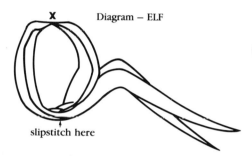

Diagram – ELF

slipstitch here

6. **Face:** From flannelette, cut a 23 mm (7/8-in) diameter circle. Run a line of gathering stitches around edge. Place button in centre. Pull up thread, enclosing button. Knot securely. Sew in place on face. Glue cheeks and eyes in place. Cut a smiling mouth from black felt and glue

in place. Fit hat on head and tack to sides of head. Glue holly leaves and berries to hat. Stitch base of ears to sides of head, close to edge of hat.

7. Fold body along fold lines into shape shown in Diagram. Slipstitch end of body to top of legs. Slipstitch centre of arms to inside of body loop at point X. Place head on top of X. Slipstitch in place. Bring arms around front of legs, just under knees. Overlap hands. Tack together. Tack hands to legs.

ELF

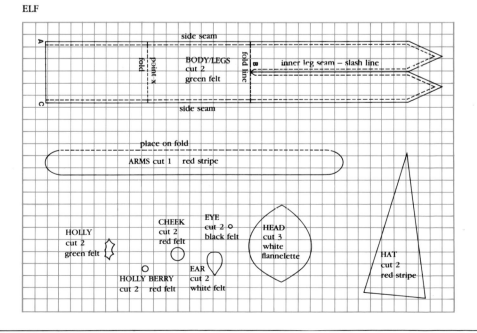

FINGER PUPPETS

This colorful cast of characters includes Santa, Mrs. Claus, Fairy Godmother, Princess, Clown, Wizard, Elf and Angel. Create a basketful of these easy-to-make puppets to sell at your bazaar, to give as gifts, or to decorate your own tree.

DESIGN BY NORENE SMILEY

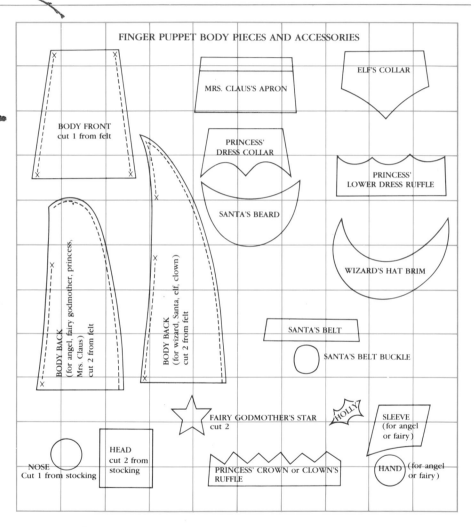

FINGER PUPPET BODY PIECES AND ACCESSORIES

MRS. CLAUS'S APRON

ELF'S COLLAR

BODY FRONT
cut 1 from felt

PRINCESS'
DRESS COLLAR

PRINCESS'
LOWER DRESS RUFFLE

SANTA'S BEARD

WIZARD'S HAT BRIM

BODY BACK
(for angel, fairy godmother, princess, Mrs. Claus)
cut 2 from felt

BODY BACK
(for wizard, Santa, elf, clown)
cut 2 from felt

SANTA'S BELT

SANTA'S BELT BUCKLE

FAIRY GODMOTHER'S STAR
cut 2

HOLLY

SLEEVE
(for angel or fairy)

NOSE
Cut 1 from stocking

HEAD
cut 2 from stocking

PRINCESS' CROWN or CLOWN'S RUFFLE

HAND (for angel or fairy)

YOU NEED:

- Felt, approx 20 cm square for each puppet body
- Scraps of felt in assorted colors
- Nylon stocking or pantyhose
- Matching threads
- Red embroidery floss
- Seed beads
- Assorted accessories and trims as follows: scraps of yarn for hair, Kurly Kate pot scrubber for fairy godmother's hair, chenille stem for

MRS. CLAUS FAIRY GODMOTHER ELF CLOWN ANGEL SANTA PRINCESS WIZARD

fairy godmother's wand, feathers for angel's wings, jingle bell for Santa's hat
• **Polyester fibrefill**
• **White craft glue**
• **Brown paper**

TO MAKE:

To enlarge pattern pieces, see General Directions (page 134).

1. Cut body front and backs from felt.

With *wrong* sides together, edgestitch one side of front to one back piece, then other side of front to other back piece between Xs. Edgestitch centre back seam and down front peak where appropriate.

2. From nylon stocking, cut 2 head pieces and 1 nose. Stitch head pieces together along 3 edges. Stuff with small pieces of fibrefill. Slipstitch opening closed. Run a line of gathering stitches around edge of nose. Place a tiny amount of fibrefill on

wrong side. Pull up gathering thread to form a small ball. Knot thread. Slipstitch to middle of face. Sew on seed bead eyes and embroider a red mouth. Pin head into body opening. Slipstitch in place.

3. Using Diagrams and photo as a guide, complete each puppet by sewing or gluing the appropriate felt accessories and hair in place. Decorate each with sequins if desired.

MR. AND MRS. CLAUS

Pleasantly plump Mr. and Mrs. Claus are so-o-o irresistible, they'll be sold out before you know it. Bespectacled Mrs. Claus wears a lacey white apron and Santa sports a jaunty red and white cap.

DESIGN BY RENÉE SCHWARZ

Finished Santa is 14 cm (5-1/2 in) high and Mrs. Claus is 7 cm (2-3/4 in) high. For full-size pattern pieces, see page 140.
Note: Sew fabric with *right sides together*, using a 6 mm (1/4-in) seam allowance throughout unless otherwise indicated. Backstitch at beginning and end of all seams.

MR. CLAUS

YOU NEED:
• **Piece of red sweat suit fleece, 26 × 20 cm (10-1/4 × 7-7/8 in), for**

body front, back, bottom and hat
• **Piece of white felt, 18 × 7 cm (7 × 2-3/4 in), for beard and hat trim**
• **Piece of flesh-tone broadcloth, 6 × 5 cm (2-3/8 × 2 in), for face**
• **White pom-pom, 16 mm in diameter**
• **Navy and red embroidery floss**
• **Matching threads**
• **Invisible nylon thread**
• **Polyester fibrefill**
• **Dressmaker's pencil**
• **Brown paper**

TO MAKE:

1. **Body:** From red fleece, cut 2 body backs, 1 body front and 1 bottom. Stitch 2 back pieces together along centre back seam, leaving a 1 cm (3/8-in) opening at top. Stitch body front to body back, leaving open at bottom and a 1 cm opening at top. Open up and pin to body bottom, matching Xs. Stitch. Turn right side out. Stuff firmly. Turn under 6 mm at top. Slipstitch opening closed.

Mr. and Mrs. Claus will be the most popular pair at any sale.

2. **Face:** Draw eyes and nose lightly on face fabric. Using a single strand of floss, embroider (satin stitch) eyes in navy and nose in red, outlining each with backstitch. Cut out face. Baste edge under 6 mm.

Pin face to body front, so bottom edge of face is approx 3 cm (1-1/8 in) up from bottom seam. Slipstitch in place, inserting a bit of stuffing behind face before closing completely.

3. **Beard:** From white felt, cut 2 beards. Stitch beard pieces together, 3 mm (1/8 in) from edge. Slipstitch beard around face and to body.

4. **Hat:** Cut hat from fleece. From felt, cut a 17 × 1 cm (6-3/4- × 3/8-in) strip. Fold hat and stitch centre back seam, leaving open at bottom. Turn right side out. Turn under 6 mm around bottom edge and hem. Stitch felt strip around bottom of hat. Sew on pom-pom. Place hat on head, matching centre back seams. Slipstitch in place.

5. Thread hanging loop of invisible thread through hat.

MRS. CLAUS

YOU NEED:
- Piece of red fleece, 26 × 20 cm (10-1/4 × 7-7/8 in) for body front, back, bottom and bonnet
- Piece of white broadcloth, 6.5 × 5 cm (2-1/2 × 2 in), for apron
- Piece of flesh-tone broadcloth, 6 × 5 cm (2-3/8 × 2 in), for face
- .20 m white bias tape, 6 mm wide
- .45 m white lace with scalloped edge, 10 mm wide
- 1 eye (i.e. hook and "eye"), 1 cm long, for glasses
- Navy red and brown embroidery floss
- Matching threads
- Invisible nylon thread
- Polyester fibrefill
- Brown paper

TO MAKE:

1. **Body:** Cut pieces from red fleece and assemble as for Mr. Claus, Step 1.

2. **Face:** Embroider features (including brown nose and red mouth); cut face from broadcloth and assemble as for Mr. Claus, Step 2. Stitch glasses in place.

3. **Bonnet:** Cut bonnet from red fleece. Turn under 6 mm around edge. Run gathering thread around edge. Stitch lace in place, so scalloped edge extends 6 mm past edge. Pull up gathering thread, so hat fits head. Knot securely. Slipstitch hat to body.

4. **Apron:** Fold apron in half, so right sides are together and short edges meet. Stitch long edge and 1 short edge. Turn right side out. Turn under 6 mm on open edge. Edgestitch around entire apron. Stitch lace to back and front of one long edge (bottom), so scalloped edge extends 3 mm past apron and ends overlap at back. Fold bias tape in half, so long edges meet. Stitch edges together. Slipstitch bias tape around body 1.5 cm above bottom seam so ends meet at centre front. Slipstitch top of apron over bias tape just under face.

5. Thread hanging loop of invisible thread through bonnet.

FOLK ART ANGEL

Wooden Folk Art Angels can be mounted on sticks as mantel or tabletop decorations, or threaded with festive ribbons and hung as tree ornaments. Make several of each for folksy, handcrafted treasures to sell at a bazaar or save as stocking stuffers.

DESIGN BY JANE BUCKLES

YOU NEED:
- Scrap of pine, 6-3/4 × 2-1/2 × 1 in, for body and feet and an additional piece, 5 × 2-1/2 × 1 in for base of angel mounted on stand
- 3/8-in dowelling, 3 in long for legs and an additional 6-1/4 in for angel mounted on stand
- Round wooden hole plug, 1-in diameter (available at most lumber and hardware stores)
- Tongue depressor
- .70 m yarn, for hair
- 9 cm coat hanger wire, for halo
- Screw eye, for hanging angel only

- .45 m ribbon
- Heavy white construction paper, watercolor paper or Bristol board
- Flesh-tone, red and blue colored pencils
- Black permanent fine-tip felt marker
- White and gold paint
- Small artist's paintbrush
- Iron-on metal stars and dots (available at craft and sewing supply stores)
- White craft glue
- Saw
- Electric drill with 1-in, 3/8-in and 1/8-in bits
- Pliers

- X-acto knife
- Sandpaper
- Brown paper

TO MAKE:

1. Cut larger piece of pine into 1 piece 6 × 2-1/2 in for body and 2 pieces 1 × 3/4 in for feet. Cut dowelling in half for legs. From tongue depressor, cut a 2-in length for arm. Sand all pieces lightly.

2. Bend one end of wire into a 1-in diameter circle and other end straight down to form stem of halo. Paint halo gold.

Folk Art Angel hung on a bough (above) or mounted on a stick (below).

3. Referring to Diagram below, drill a 1-in hole in front of body for face, two 3/8-in holes in opposite end of body for legs, one 3/8-in hole in each foot to fit legs, seven 1/8-in holes around face for hair and one 1/8-in hole in top of block above face for halo.

4. From paper, cut out 2 of each wing layer and 1 hand (shown actual size on page 142). Referring to Diagram, glue one set of wings one layer on top of the other to front of body and the other set to back. Glue arm and hand in place.

5. Glue plug in face hole and legs into body and feet.

6. Color face with flesh-tone pencil. Draw features with marker and other pencils. Rub with finger to soften look if necessary. Paint all other parts white. Paint decorative dots, stars and wavy lines on body with gold paint or decorate with iron-on shapes following manufacturer's directions for ironing onto fabric.

7. Cut yarn into seven 10 cm (4-in) lengths. Fold each in half. Dab glue on

fold and poke into each hole around face with nail or darning needle. When glue is dry, trim hair. Glue halo in hole in top of head.

8. To hang angel, insert screw eye into centre top of body, thread loop of ribbon through it and tie in a bow. To mount angel on base, omit screw eye. Drill one 3/8-in hole in bottom of block under arm and another in base. Glue and insert extra dowel in holes. Tie ribbon bow around base of dowel.

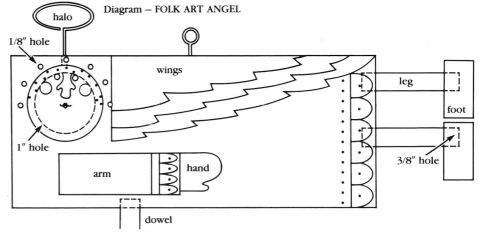

Diagram – FOLK ART ANGEL

halo
1/8″ hole
1″ hole
wings
leg
foot
3/8″ hole
arm
hand
dowel

Canadian Living

GLORIOUS CHRISTMAS CRAFTS

DOLLS AND TOYS TO MAKE

CHAPTER VI

PAWS

Paws is a cuddly armful of adorable bear to create for that special child who'll give him lots of love. He's fake fur on the outside and inside he's all heart and polyester fibrefill. A minimum number of pattern pieces makes it an easy-to-sew project.

DESIGN BY ANNA HOBBS

YOU NEED:
- **.80 m beige fake fur, 140 cm wide**
- **Piece of dark brown felt, 25 cm (9-7/8 in) square**
- **Scrap of black felt**
- **Matching thread**
- **1 m dark brown yarn**
- **1 m ribbon, 25 mm wide**
- **Polyester fibrefill**
- **Water-soluble fabric marker**
- **White craft glue**
- **Brown paper**

TO MAKE:
To enlarge pattern, see General Directions (page 134).
Note: Use a 13 mm (1/2-in) seam allowance throughout.

1. From brown felt, cut 2 paws, 2 soles and 2 large eye circles. From black felt, cut 2 small eye circles.

2. Place remaining pattern pieces on wrong side of single thickness of fake fur, positioning each piece so arrow runs in direction of nap. To determine direction of nap, stroke fur in whichever direction will make it lie flat and feel smoothest. Trace around pattern pieces with marker, being careful to reverse pattern pieces for arms and legs. Cut out pieces. Use tip of scissors only to snip through fabric backing, being careful not to cut fur on right side.

3. Topstitch felt paw pads in place on fur side of one right and one left arm. With right sides together, stitch arm pieces together in pairs, leaving open at top. Trim seam allowances. Clip curves. Turn right side out. Stuff arms firmly to within 2.5 cm (1 in) of top. Machine-stitch closed.

4. With right sides together, stitch leg pieces together in pairs down centre front and centre back seams. With right sides together and notches matching leg seams, stitch felt sole to bottom of each foot. Trim seam allowances. Clip corners and curves. Turn right side out. Stuff legs firmly to within 2.5 cm of top. Fold top of leg so that front and back seams align. Machine-stitch closed.

5. With right sides together, stitch ear pieces together in pairs, leaving open where indicated. Trim seam allowances. Clip curves. Turn right side out. Do not stuff. Baste raw edges together, pulling thread up slightly to gather edge.

6. With raw edges even, baste ears to right side of body front where indicated.

With right sides together, stitch body front to body back from one shoulder, around head to opposite shoulder, catching ears in stitching. Insert arms between front and back body so raw end of each arm is even with raw edge of side seam and so paws point upward. Stitch side seams, catching arms in stitching.

7. With right sides together and toes pointing away from body, stitch raw end of legs to bottom edge of body back. Turn body right side out. Stuff head and body firmly, filling out cheeks and shoulders as much as possible. Slipstitch bottom opening closed.

8. **Snout:** Run a line of gathering stitches around edge of snout circle. Place a

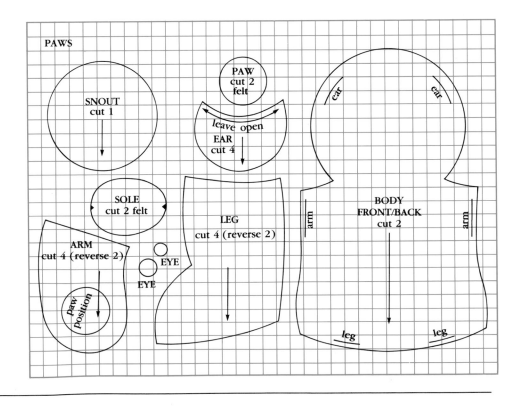

handful of fibrefill on wrong side. Pull up gathering thread, adjusting stuffing to form a ball. Knot threads. Flatten snout slightly. Glue then slipstitch in place on face.

9. **Face:** With dark brown yarn,

embroider nose and smiling mouth as shown in photo. Appliqué black eye circles on larger brown eye circles. With white thread, embroider 2 small stitches for highlight on each eye. Glue then

slipstitch eyes in place on either side of snout.

10. Comb all seams so they are concealed by fur pile.

YUM YUM

*He looks like a cute cookie, but this gingerbread man is made of felt.
Simply cut him out, stitch on the jumbo rickrack to look like icing, and then glue on his face
and buttons. Once you've stitched his front and back together, he's ready for stuffing.*

DESIGN BY ANNA HOBBS

Finished gingerbread man stands 62 cm (24-3/8 in) tall.

YOU NEED:
- **.50 m brown felt, 180 cm wide**
- **Scraps of colored felt for eyes, nose, mouth and buttons**
- **3 m jumbo white rickrack**
- **.90 m red ribbon, 23 mm wide**
- **Polyester fibrefill**
- **White craft glue**
- **Brown paper**

TO MAKE:
To enlarge pattern, see General Directions (page 134).

1. Cut 2 gingerbread men from brown felt.

2. Starting and ending at crotch, machine-stitch rickrack 2.5 cm (1 in) in from edge of front. Cut eyes, nose, mouth and buttons from felt scraps. Glue in place.

3. With wrong sides together, edgestitch front to back, leaving open between notches. Stuff. Stitch opening closed. Tie ribbon around neck.

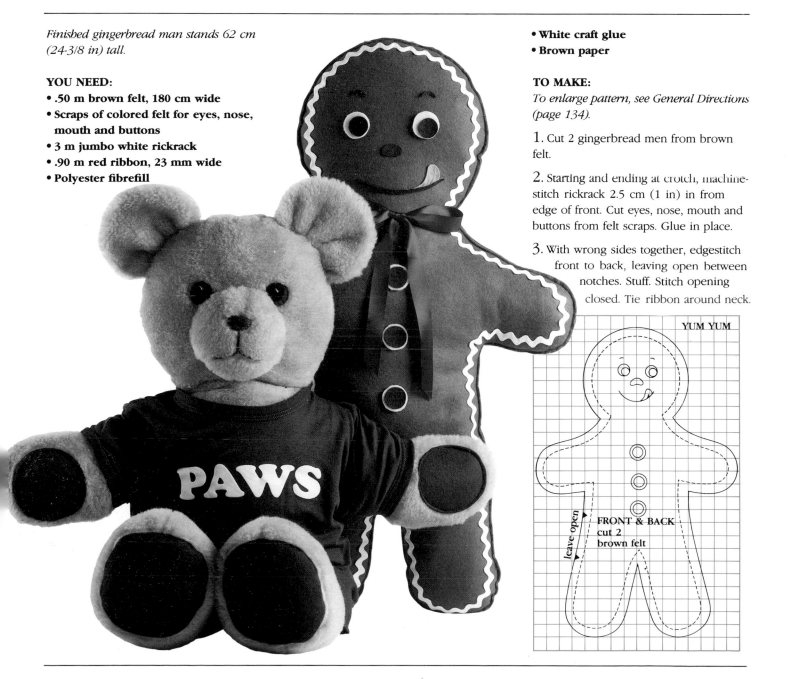

YUM YUM

FRONT & BACK
cut 2
brown felt

leave open

107

HENDERSON BEAR

For the teddy bear lover in all of us, here is a lovable, huggable and movable teddy perfect for Christmas gift-giving. Joint discs inserted in the neck and at the shoulders and hips mean Henderson Bear can sit, "walk" and most of all, hug you right back.

DESIGN BY HELEN HENDERSON

Finished bear is approx 40 cm (15-3/4 in) tall.

YOU NEED:

- .50 m camel-colored fake fur with 1 cm (3/8-in) pile, 150 cm wide
- Piece of imitation suede, 15 cm (6 in) square
- Brown embroidery thread
- Matching thread
- Buttonhole twist thread
- 2 brown lock-in eyes, 15 mm in diameter
- 4 doll joints, 30 mm in diameter
- 1 doll joint, 45 mm in diameter
- Embroidery needle
- Polyester fibrefill
- Water-soluble fabric marker
- Brown paper

TO MAKE:

To enlarge pattern, see General Directions (page 134).

Note: Use a 6 mm (1/4-in) seam allowance throughout, unless otherwise indicated. Backstitch at beginning and end of seams.

1. From imitation suede, cut 2 paws (reversing 1) and 2 soles.

2. Place remaining pattern pieces on wrong side of single thickness of fake fur, positioning each piece so arrow runs in direction of nap. To determine direction of nap, stroke fur in whichever direction will make it lie flat and feel smoothest. Trace around pattern pieces with marker, being careful to reverse pattern pieces for body, arms, legs and sides. Transfer

all pattern markings. Cut out pieces. Use tip of scissors only to snip through fabric backing, being careful not to cut fur on right side.

3. Stitch darts on each head side. With right sides together, stitch head sides together from A to B. With right sides together, pin head crest to head sides matching points A and C on each piece. Stitch around head crest from C to A to C on opposite side. Clip curves. Turn head right side out. Cut small eye holes in face as indicated. Insert eye shanks. Lock in place on wrong side.

4. Stuff head firmly. With buttonhole twist, run a gathering thread around neck opening. Insert 45 mm joint disc with post into neck opening. Pull gathers tight around disc, allowing post to stick out of neck opening. Tie thread securely.

5. With right sides together, stitch 2 ear pieces, leaving open where indicated. Clip curves. Turn right side out. Topstitch ear opening closed. Trim close to topstitching. Repeat for second ear. Pin ears to head at positions indicated. Using buttonhole twist, slipstitch ears securely in place.

6. With brown floss and using satin stitch, embroider nose and mouth.

7. Pierce very small holes in both body pieces for arm and leg joints.

8. With right sides of body pieces together, stitch from D to E and from F to G. With buttonhole twist, run a gathering thread around neck opening. Pull gathers tight and tie threads securely. Turn body right side out.

9. Position head on top of body, pushing post from head disc through hole in neck gathers of body. Slip washer onto post, then push locking washer up post as far as it will go. Joint must be tight.

10. With right sides together and straight edges even, stitch suede paw to inner arm. Pierce small hole in inner arm for arm joint. With right sides together, stitch outer arm to inner arm, leaving open at top where indicated. Clip curves. Turn right side out. Stuff arm firmly to joint hole.
Repeat for second arm.

11. Making sure that arms are on correct side of body and are facing forward, insert 30 mm joint disc with post from inside of each arm through hole in arm and corresponding hole in body. On inside of body, slip washers onto posts then push locking washers up posts as far as possible.

12. Finish stuffing arms and slipstitch openings closed.

13. With right sides of 2 legs together, stitch from H to J and from K to L. Clip corner and curves. With right sides together and notches matching seam lines, stitch suede sole to bottom of foot. Pierce a small hole on inside of leg for joint. Stuff leg firmly up to joint hole. Repeat for second leg, making sure to pierce hole in opposite inner leg so you will have a left and right leg.

14. Attach legs to body as given for arms in Step 11.

15. Finish stuffing legs and slipstitch openings closed.

16. Stuff body firmly, putting lots of stuffing around joints to pad them. Slipstitch opening G-E closed.

17. Comb all seams so they are concealed by fur pile.

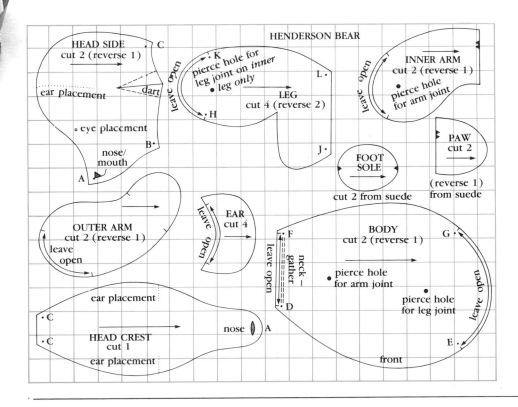

MERRY MARY

Make a child's Christmas dream come true with the gift of a precious doll.
Merry Mary is fun to sew. Included are patterns for her nightgown, dust
cap and boots. She's definitely a cuddly charmer.

DESIGN BY DENISE FLYS

Finished doll is 56 cm (22 in) tall.

YOU NEED:

For body:

- .60 m flesh-tone broadcloth, 115 cm wide
- 1 ball (25 g) dark brown mohair yarn, for hair
- Scrap of brown felt, for eyes
- Brown thread, for mouth
- Polyester fibrefill

For clothes:

- 1.50 m flannelette, 115 cm wide
- 1 m satin ribbon, 10 mm wide
- 1 m lingerie elastic
- 2 snap fasteners

TO MAKE:

To enlarge pattern, see General Directions (page 134).

Note: Sew fabric with right sides together, using a 6 mm (1/4-in) seam allowance throughout.

BODY

1. From flesh-tone broadcloth, cut body front, 2 body backs, 4 arms and 4 legs.

2. **Arms:** With right sides together, stitch 2 arm pieces together, leaving open at top. Turn right side out. Stuff hand only enough to give a little thickness to fingers. Topstitch along finger lines as shown on pattern. Continue stuffing to broken line (elbow). Topstitch along this line. This makes the arm flexible. Stuff upper arm and machine-stitch closed. Repeat for second arm.

3. **Legs:** With right sides together, stitch 2 leg pieces together, leaving open at top. Turn right side out. Stuff to broken line (knee). Fold leg so front and back seams align. Topstitch along knee line. This makes the leg flexible. Stuff upper leg and machine-stitch closed. Repeat for second leg.

4. **Body:** With right sides together, stitch body back pieces together along centre back seam. Stitch body front to body back around head from point A on one side to point A on opposite side. Reinforce stitching at corners. Clip.

Insert arms between front and back pieces (right sides still together) so top of each arm is even with raw edge of side seam between A and B and so hands point down toward centre of body. Stitch side seams, catching arms in stitching. Turn body right side out.

With right sides together and raw edges even, stitch top of legs to bottom edge of body back making sure feet will point forward. Stuff head and body firmly. Slipstitch bottom opening closed.

5. Hair: Cut 27 strands of yarn, each 90 cm (35-1/2 in) long. Tie bundle of yarn in middle and sew securely to doll's forehead at X shown on pattern. Smooth over each side of head, framing face. Gather together hair about halfway down each side of head and sew to large dots indicated on pattern. Braid remainder of strands and tie at ends. Cut a piece of cardboard 35 cm (13-7/8 in) long. Wind yarn around it 55 times. Do not cut. Before removing from card, tie loops together through centre of bundle. Sew this point to top of head, just behind hair already in place. Smooth evenly around back and sides of head. Tack ends of loops in place along back of neck to look like curls.

6. Face: Cut small circles of brown felt for eyes. Sew in place. Embroider a smile with a single strand of brown thread.

DUST CAP

1. With right sides together, stitch cap pieces together, leaving a 7 cm (2-3/4-in) opening where indicated. Turn right side out. Press.

2. To form casing, topstitch 5 cm (2 in) from outer edge. Topstitch 1 cm outside this line, leaving a small opening at same point where seam has been left open. Insert elastic through these openings and through casing. Pull up to fit doll's head and sew ends of elastic together. Topstitch casing opening closed. Slipstitch seam opening closed.

3. Tie a small ribbon bow and attach to front of cap.

NIGHTGOWN

1. From flannelette, cut nightgown front (on fold), 2 backs, 2 sleeves, 2 yoke fronts, 2 right back yokes, 2 left back yokes, 1 strip 51 × 7.5 cm (20-1/8 × 3 in) for neck ruffle, 1 strip 96 × 5 cm (37-7/8 × 2 in) for yoke ruffle and 2 strips each 96 × 12.5 cm (37-7/8 × 5 in) for hem ruffle. Also cut 2 dust cap and 4 boot pieces.

2. Stitch front and back yokes together at shoulders. Repeat with remaining yoke pieces for yoke facing.

3. Fold neck ruffle in half so right sides are together and long edges meet. Stitch

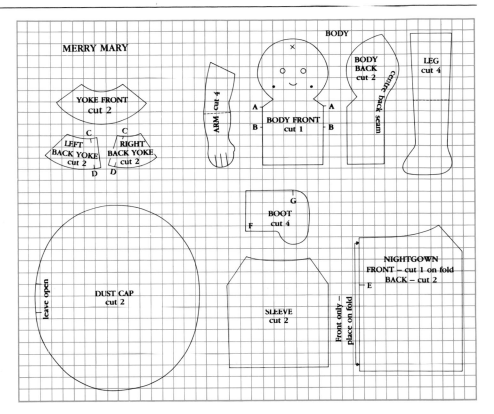

ends. Turn right side out. Press. Run a line of gathering stitches down raw edge, 6 mm from edge. Pull up thread and pin ruffle to neck edge of yoke between C and C, adjusting gathers to fit. Baste.

4. Narrowly hem one long edge and both ends of yoke ruffle. Gather raw edge and with right sides together, pin to lower edge of yoke between D and D, adjusting gathers to fit. Baste.

5. With right sides together, stitch yoke facing to yoke down centre back edges and around neck. Turn right side out. Press.

6. Stitch back pieces together from bottom edge to E. Turn under and hem centre back opening edges.

7. Stitch sleeves to front and back of nightgown at raglan seams. Gather top edge of front/back and with right sides together, pin around lower edge of yoke (do not pin to facing), matching centre of sleeve to yoke shoulder seam and adjusting gathers evenly to fit. Stitch. Turn under lower edge of yoke facing and slipstitch in place. Sew snap fasteners to right and left back yoke edges.

8. Turn under 6 mm then 3 cm (1-1/8 in)

along bottom of each sleeve. Topstitch close to first fold, then 1 cm (3/8 in) from this to form casing. Insert elastic and secure at one end of casing. Pull up to fit around doll's wrist and secure at other end of casing. Thread elastic through other sleeve in same manner. Stitch sleeve and side seams.

9. Stitch short ends of 2 hem ruffle strips together to form a loop. Narrowly hem both edges. Gather 2 cm (3/4 in) from one edge. Lap gathered edge of ruffle 2.5 cm (1 in) over bottom edge of nightgown. Pin in place, adjusting gathers to fit. Topstitch along gathering line.

10. Tie a small ribbon bow and attach to front neck.

BOOTS

1. With right sides together, stitch 2 boot pieces together from F to G.

2. Turn under 6 mm then 1 cm around top of boot. Topstitch close to first fold. Insert elastic through casing. Pull up to fit doll's ankle and secure at both ends. Make second boot in same manner.

3. Stitch remaining section of centre back seams closed.

MY TWIN DOLL

Why not sew an adorable look-alike for the favorite boy or girl on your Christmas list? A life-size companion to dress up in matching clothes can be as individual as the little person it's made for.

DESIGN BY BEVERLEY PLAXTON

YOU NEED:

- **1 m flesh-tone broadcloth, 115 cm wide**
- **Scraps of felt for eyes and shoes**
- **Ball of yarn for hair**
- **Thread to match body, eyes, hair and shoes**
- **White, dark brown and pink embroidery floss**
- **Polyester fibrefill**
- **Paper towel roll, for neck support**
- **Orange felt-tip permanent marker, for freckles (optional)**
- **Water-soluble fabric marker**
- **White craft glue**
- **Brown paper**

TO MAKE:

To enlarge pattern, see General Directions (page 134). To alter doll's height, lengthen or shorten at double line indicated on body and leg pieces.

Note: Cut out body pieces after stitching seams as described below.

1. Fold broadcloth in half so right sides are together and long raw edges meet. Lay pattern pieces for body, arms (twice), legs (twice) and ears (twice) at least 2.5 cm (1 in) apart on fabric. With fabric marker, trace around each; this is the sewing line. Do not cut out. Place pins around each piece at right angles to sewing line to hold the layers together. Using a closely spaced machine stitch, sew pieces together along marked lines, leaving bottom of body, top of legs and arms and straight edge of ears open.

2. Cut out all pieces, leaving a 6 mm (1/4-in) seam allowance around each. Clip corners and curves, especially around fingers. Turn pieces right side out. Roll seams between fingers to smooth edges. With fabric marker, lightly mark finger lines on right side of hands. Topstitch along these lines.

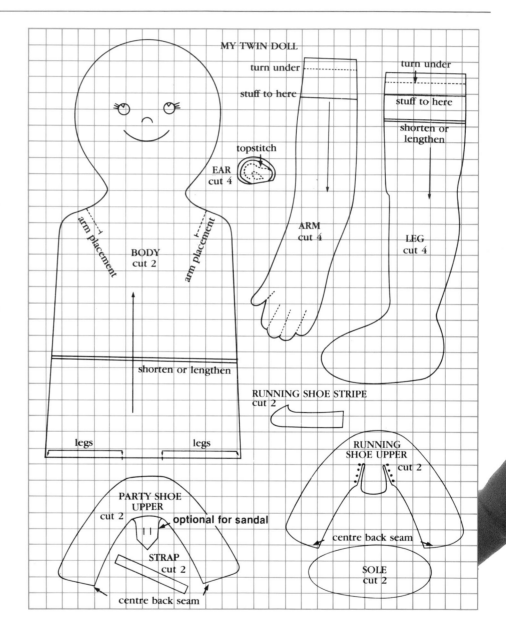

3. Stuff head firmly, shaping round face as you go. Insert paper towel roll halfway into centre of head. Stuff neck around roll. Stuff body firmly. Turn under raw edges and slipstitch closed.

4. Stuff arms and legs to level indicated on pattern. Turn under 15 mm (5/8 in) around top edge of arms and legs. Using double thread, slipstitch legs to body where indicated. Pin top of each arm over front and back of each shoulder along placement line. Slipstitch securely in place.

5. Face: Lightly mark facial features on face. Cut small circles of felt for eyes. With 6 strands of white floss, embroider highlight on each eye. Slipstitch eyes in place. With a single strand of brown floss, embroider eyelashes. Using outline stitch and 6 strands of pink floss, embroider nose and mouth. If desired, dot freckles on cheeks with orange marker (test on scrap of fabric first).

6. Hair: For long hair, measure length from one shoulder, over head to opposite shoulder. Wind yarn into a hank this

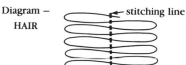

Diagram – HAIR ← stitching line

length and as thick as you wish the hair to be. For loose hairdo, lay hank out to a width of 5 to 10 cm (2 to 4 in). For hair drawn up in pigtails, lay hank out to a width of 20.5 cm (8 in). With matching thread, stitch hair part across centre of hank (see Diagram). For curly ends, leave ends of yarn in loops. For straight hair or pigtails, cut loops. Arrange

hair on doll's head so part starts on forehead, 4 cm (1-5/8 in) below head seam. Sew part to head. For bangs, trim front hair above eyes. Glue a layer of hair to scalp. Arrange hairdo. For short curly hair, wrap yarn around 5 cm (2-in) wide strips of paper. Machine-stitch down centre of paper and wound yarn. Remove paper. Make as many strips of curls as necessary to achieve desired amount and thickness of hair. Sew clusters of curls over doll's head. Separate and fluff out loops.

7. Ears: Stuff ears lightly. Tuck raw edges to inside. Topstitch along broken lines. Slipstitch ears in place on either side of head along seam lines.

8. Clothes: Dress doll in ready-made clothes or sew clothes from size 3 commercial patterns.

9. Shoes: From felt, cut 2 shoe uppers, 2 soles and appropriate trim (i.e. 2 straps for party shoes or sandals and 2 stripes for running shoes). Whipstitch or machine-stitch centre back seam, using a minimal seam allowance. Stitch sole to bottom of shoe in same manner. Turn shoe right side out if desired. Glue stripe to outside of each running shoe. Lace up shoes with strong thread. Sew strap across top of foot on party shoes and sandals.

Canadian Living

GLORIOUS CHRISTMAS CRAFTS

GIFTS TO MAKE

CHAPTER
VII

HOSTESS GIFTS

During the holiday season or any time of the year, delight your favorite host or hostess with a thoughtful, handmade gift. It's one of the most individual ways to say "thank you." Here are eight ideas — from a windowsill herb garden to cinnamon-scented fire-starters — varied and versatile enough to appeal to many tastes and interests.

Scented Fire-Starters and Fireplace Mitts (instructions, p. 118).

PERSONALIZED CHRISTMAS TREE ORNAMENT

Design by Jean Scobie

YOU NEED:

- **Piece of balsa wood, 3 × 3 × 1/8 in**
- **X-acto knife or utility knife**
- **Extra fine sandpaper or emery board**
- **Drill with 1/16-in bit**
- **Urethane**
- **Model paint**
- **Fine artist's paintbrush**
- **Permanent fine-tip felt marker**
- **Thread to hang ornament**

TO MAKE:

1. Transfer outline of house (shown actual size on page 142) onto balsa wood. Cut out with X-acto knife. Drill hole in chimney. Sand edges smooth.

2. Apply one coat of urethane to both sides of house. Let dry. Sand lightly.

3. With model paint and using pattern as a guide, paint one side of the house, then, when completely dry, paint the other. Write recipient's name across the front with marker. Let dry.

4. Apply a second coat of urethane. Let dry. Attach hanging thread

Personalized Christmas Tree Ornament.

SCENTED FIRE-STARTERS

YOU NEED:

- **Christmas paper baking cups**
- **Sawdust**
- **Oil of cinnamon (available at drugstores and specialty food shops)**
- **Paraffin wax or old candles**

TO MAKE:

1. Line muffin tins with paper baking cups. Fill each three-quarters full with sawdust. Add a drop of oil of cinnamon to each.

2. Melt paraffin wax or old candles in top of double boiler. Allow approx 50 mL (1/4 cup) of wax per muffin tin. Pour over sawdust. Let stand.

3. When cool and hardened, starters are ready for use. Package as desired with instructions to place two or three beneath kindling and logs in the fireplace.

WINDOWSILL HERBS AND MARKERS

Design by Jean Scobie

YOU NEED:

- **Potted herb plants**
  or **herb seeds (such as parsley, chives, thyme), potting soil and clay pots**
- **Piece of balsa wood, 8 × 1 × 1/8 in, for each marker**
- **X-acto or utility knife**
- **Extra fine sandpaper or emery board**
- **Urethane**
- **Model paint**
- **Fine artist's paintbrush**
- **Permanent fine-tip felt marker**

TO MAKE:

1. With X-acto knife, round off top corners of balsa-wood stick and cut bottom to a long point. Sand edges smooth.

2. Paint stick with urethane. Let dry. Sand lightly.

3. With model paint, paint simple drawing of herb at top of one side of stick, using illustration on seed packet or in nursery catalogue as a guide. With marker, write

Windowsill Herbs and Markers.

name of herb beneath this. Let dry.

4. Apply a second coat of urethane. Let dry.

5. Poke markers into herb plants or package together with seeds, soil and pots.

Oven-To-Table Mitts.

OVEN-TO-TABLE MITTS

YOU NEED:

- **Pair of oven mitts**
- **.40 m white quilted eyelet fabric, 115 cm wide**
- **.75 m eyelet lace trim, 45 mm wide, ruffled along both edges and suitable for threading a narrow ribbon through the centre**
- **1 m red ribbon, 5 mm wide**
- **Brown paper**

TO MAKE:

1. Trace outline of oven mitt onto brown paper. Add 13 mm (1/2 in) to all edges for ease and seam allowance.

2. With right sides of fabric together, cut out 2 mitt shapes for each mitt (4 in all).

3. With right sides together and using a 6 mm (1/4-in) seam allowance, sew 2

mitt pieces together, leaving top edge open. Clip curves. Turn right side out. Repeat with other 2 pieces.

4. Baste under 6 mm around top edge of each mitt. Sew eyelet trim around top edge. Thread ribbon through centre of trim and tie ends in a bow. Insert mitts into eyelet covers.

FIREPLACE MITTS

Follow instructions for Oven-to-Table Mitts (above), substituting black velveteen for quilted eyelet fabric and metallic trim, 10 mm wide for eyelet trim and ribbon.

QUILTED CASSEROLE COVER

YOU NEED:
• **Oval casserole dish**
• **Pre-quilted fabric**
• **Co-ordinating extra wide double-fold bias tape**
• **Matching thread**
• **Water-soluble fabric marker**

TO MAKE:

1. Trace around bottom of casserole dish onto wrong side of quilted fabric. Add 2.5 cm (1 in) to all edges for ease. Cut out. For sides, cut a rectangle, the length equal to the circumference of the dish × the depth of the dish + 6 cm (2-3/8 in). Cut rectangle in half so you have 2 sides.

2. Bind 1 long and 2 short edges of each side piece. With *wrong* sides together and using a 6 mm (1/4-in) seam allowance, centre and stitch raw edge of each side piece to long curved edge on either side of bottom. Bind bottom edge.

3. Topstitch edges of a 1.20 m (47-1/4-in) length of bias tape together. Cut into 4 pieces for ties. Sew ties to top corners of sides. Fill dish with recipe ingredients, insert in quilted cover and tie closed.

BIRD FEEDER

YOU NEED:
• **Small cedar, fir or hardwood tree branch, 4-in diameter, approx 12 in long**
• **1/4-in dowelling, 36 in long**
• **1/4-in screw eye, approx 3 in long**
• **Electric drill with 1/4-in and 1-in bits**
• **Wood glue**
• **10 in thick plastic-covered wire**
• **Bird food and suet**

TO MAKE:

1. Drill 12 to 20, 1-in holes, 1 in deep, spaced at random around the branch. Drill a 1/4-in hole, 1/4 in deep, 1 in below each large hole.

2. Cut dowelling into 2-1/2-in long pieces. Glue these into small holes. Insert screw eye into top of branch. Loop wire through eye to hang.

3. Mix bird food with suet and pack into large holes.

CHAPS APRON

YOU NEED:
• **1.20 m denim or sturdy cotton, 115 cm wide**
• **Contrasting colored buttonhole twist thread**
• **Brown paper**

Fill a quilt-covered casserole dish with pasta favorites.

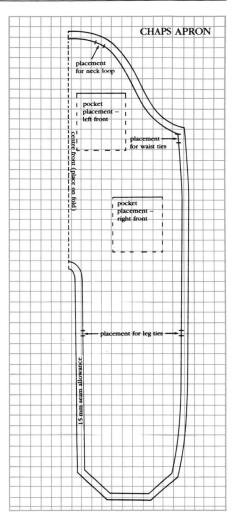

CHAPS APRON

placement for neck loop

pocket placement – left front

placement for waist ties

centre front (place on fold)

pocket placement – right front

placement for leg ties

15 mm seam allowance

Your host will love the Chaps Apron.

TO MAKE:

To enlarge pattern, see General Directions (page 134).
Note: All stitching is done with buttonhole thread and a long machine stitch to give a saddle stitch effect.

1. Fold fabric in half lengthwise. Place pattern on fold and cut out apron. Also cut 2 strips, each 100 × 5 cm (39-3/8 × 2 in) for leg ties, 3 strips, each 65 × 10 cm (25-5/8 × 4 in) for waist ties and neck loop and 2 pockets, each 17 × 14 cm (6-3/4 × 5-1/2 in).

2. Press under 6 mm (1/4 in) then 10 mm (3/8 in) on all edges of apron. Topstitch.

3. Press under 3 mm (1/8 in) on long edges of tie strips. Fold each strip in half so long edges meet. Topstitch 3 mm from both long edges. Cut leg ties in half. Stitch 2 ties to wrong side of each leg where indicated. Stitch waist ties to either side of apron and neck loop to either side of neck edge (adjust length to fit if necessary).

4. Press under 3 mm on all edges of pockets. Then press under a 2.5 cm (1-in) hem on one short edge of each pocket (top). Topstitch hem. Topstitch pockets in place.

LUXURIOUS GIFTS

A lot of luxury for a little price... With a bit of time and imagination, you can turn fine fabrics and flea-market finds into exquisite, one-of-a-kind, handmade presents. Satin is the perfect choice for a dainty Camisole, Half Slip and matching Lingerie Bag. Rich-looking velvet added to an antique napkin ring becomes an elegant Pincushion or Earring Holder. Vintage coins, buttons and beads can be worked into unique Cuff Links, Stickpins and Necklaces. A satin-covered Jewelry Box or suede Accessory Box can store these treasures. Marbleized Shaker Boxes and Gift Boxes make lovely packages for handmade gifts. All are elegant ways to say "I care."

DESIGNS BY CAROLYN SMITH

PINCUSHION

YOU NEED:
- **Piece of purple velvet, 15 cm (6 in) square**
- **Piece of black felt, 5 cm (2 in) square**
- **Napkin ring**
- **Piece of lightweight cardboard, 5 cm square**
- **Heavy thread**
- **Polyester fibrefill**
- **White craft glue**
- **Geometry compass**
- **Dressmaker's chalk**

TO MAKE:

1. Using compass, draw a 13 cm (5-1/8-in) diameter circle on wrong side of velvet. Cut out. Run a line of gathering stitches around edge of circle. Place a handful of fibrefill on wrong side. Pull up gathering thread, adjusting stuffing to form a ball (ball should be slightly larger in diameter than napkin ring). Check size and firmness of ball by pushing into ring. Adjust if necessary. Knot thread.

2. Apply glue to inside of ring. Push ball into ring, smooth side up. Let dry.

3. Trace around ring onto cardboard. Cut out. Trim circle to fit into bottom of ring. Glue around edge of circle and insert into bottom of ring.

4. Trace around ring onto felt. Cut out. Glue felt circle to cardboard at bottom of ring.

EARRING HOLDER

YOU NEED:
- **Piece of purple velvet, 18 × 10 cm (7 × 4 in)**
- **Piece of black felt, 5 cm (2 in) square**
- **Napkin ring**
- **Lightweight cardboard**
- **White craft glue**
- **Dressmaker's chalk**

TO MAKE:

1. Trace around napkin ring onto cardboard. Cut out. Trim circle to fit into bottom of ring. Trace around ring onto wrong side of velvet. Draw a line 2 cm (3/4 in) outside traced line (for folding allowance). Cut out. Centre and glue cardboard circle to wrong side of velvet circle. Cut several notches in folding allowance and fold around cardboard. Glue in place. Glue around edge of covered circle and insert into bottom of ring so right side faces up inside the ring.

2. Trace around ring onto felt. Cut out. Glue felt circle to covered cardboard at bottom of ring.

An array of one-of-a-kind gifts: (clockwise from top left) Marbleized Shaker Boxes (p. 126),
Jewelry Box (p. 124), Cuff Links (p. 122), Bead Necklaces (p. 122), Moiré Mouse (p. 122), Lingerie Bag (p. 122),
Camisole (p. 123), Half Slip (p. 123), Earring Holder (p. 120) and Pincushion (p. 120) with Stick Pins (p. 122).

3. Measure inside depth of napkin ring. Cut a cardboard strip approx 20 cm (7-7/8 in) long × depth. Fit strip around inside of ring and trim so ends are 3 mm (1/8 in) short of meeting. Trace around cardboard strip onto wrong side of velvet. Draw lines 1 cm (3/8 in) outside traced lines (for folding allowance). Cut out. Centre and glue cardboard strip to wrong side of velvet strip. Cut notches in folding allowance at each corner and fold around cardboard. Glue in place. Apply glue to inside of ring. Fit covered strip around inside of ring. Let dry.

CUFF LINKS

YOU NEED:
- **Metal or plastic buttons, or old coins**
- **Cuff-link backings (purchased or pried off old or inexpensive cuff links)**
- **Nail file or emery board**
- **Fast-bonding "instant" glue**
- **Pliers**

TO MAKE:

1. With pliers, snip wire shanks off metal buttons. File plastic loops off plastic buttons.

2. Glue cuff-link backings to back of buttons or coins, holding in place with pliers until glue sets. Reinforce around join with extra glue.

BEAD NECKLACE

YOU NEED:
- **Assorted beads and pendants (purchased or from old jewelry)**
- **Tiger tail wire (nylon-covered beading wire) or nylon fishing line**
- **Necklace clasp**
- **Pliers**

TO MAKE:

1. Cover work area with cloth or towel to prevent beads from rolling.

2. Cut a length of beading wire slightly longer than desired length of finished necklace. Thread beads, starting arrangement at centre and working out

to both ends.

3. Tie one half of clasp securely to each end as close as possible to last bead.

STICKPIN

YOU NEED:
- **Beads or shank-type buttons**
- **Corsage pin**
- **Fast-bonding "instant" glue**
- **Pliers**

TO MAKE:
If using beads: Snip off head of pin. Thread one or more beads onto pin and glue in place at cut end. Or if you wish, leave head of pin in place and add beads below it.
If using buttons: Snip off head of pin. Glue and insert cut end into shank of button.

MOIRÉ MOUSE

YOU NEED:
- **Piece of white polyester moiré taffeta, 28 × 11 cm (11 × 4-3/8 in)**
- **15 cm satin cord**
- **Matching thread**
- **Small amount of polyester fibrefill**
- **Small amount of potpourri**
- **Brown paper**

TO MAKE:
To enlarge pattern, see General Directions (page 134).
Note: Use a 6 mm (1/4-in) seam allowance throughout.

1. From taffeta, cut body/head and ear pieces. With right sides together, stitch 3 body/head pieces together, leaving a 2.5 cm (1-in) opening at centre of one seam. Clip curves. Turn right side out.

2. Stuff body/head with fibrefill. Poke a small hole in centre of fibrefill and fill with potpourri. Cover hole with fibrefill. Slipstitch opening closed (bottom edge of mouse).

3. With right sides together, stitch 2 ears together, leaving straight edge open. Clip curves. Turn right side out. Press. Turn under 3 mm (1/8 in) around open

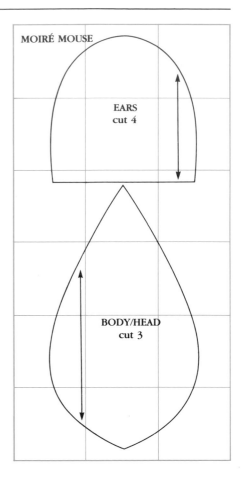

MOIRÉ MOUSE

EARS
cut 4

BODY/HEAD
cut 3

end. Run a line of gathering stitches through both layers, close to folded edge. Pull up thread so gathered edge is 1.5 cm (5/8 in) long. Knot thread. Make second ear in same manner. Stitch gathered edge of ears to head, approx 1.5 cm from tip of nose.

4. Snip a few stitches open at tail end of mouse. Poke in one end of cord, for tail. Slipstitch opening closed, securing cord at same time. Knot end of tail.

LINGERIE BAG

YOU NEED:
- **.80 m satin, 115 cm wide**
- **Piece of compressed polyester batting (such as Thermolam), 62 × 37 cm (24-3/8 × 14-5/8 in)**
- **Matching thread**

TO MAKE:
Note: Use a 6 mm (1/4-in) seam allowance throughout.

1. From satin, cut a 63 × 38 cm

(24-7/8- × 15-in) rectangle for inside of bag and a 75 × 38 cm (29-1/2- × 15-in) rectangle for outside of bag.

2. **Outside bag:** On right side, beginning 2 cm (3/4 in) from one short edge of large rectangle, make three 2 cm pleats, 2 cm apart, parallel to short edge (fold toward short edge). Baste pleats along long edges. Centre batting on wrong side of pleated rectangle. Baste around edges.

3. With right sides together, stitch rectangle for inside bag to outside rectangle, leaving a 7.5 cm (3-in) opening at centre of short edge opposite pleats. Turn right side out. Remove basting. Press. Turn under 6 mm around opening and slipstitch closed.

4. Fold unpleated end of rectangle up 20 cm (7-7/8 in) toward inside, forming bag. Hand-stitch side seams on inside. Fold pleated end (flap) over bag.

5. From satin, cut 2 strips 35 × 5 cm (13-7/8 × 2 in), for ties. Fold each strip in half so right sides are together and long edges meet. Stitch across one end and up long open edge on each tie. Turn right side out. Press.
Snip a few stitches open at centre of pleated edge of flap. Poke in raw end of one tie. Slipstitch opening closed, securing tie at same time. Turn under 6 mm around open end of second tie. Slipstitch closed. Hand-stitch to centre of bottom edge of bag.

CAMISOLE

YOU NEED:
- **.80 m satin, 115 cm wide**
- **1 m lace, 50 mm wide**
- **Matching threads**
- **String**
- **Brown paper**

TO MAKE:
Draw and cut pattern from brown paper, following measurements for size Small (S), Medium (M) or Large (L) on Diagrams that follow.
Note: To enclose raw edges, sew French seam as follows: With wrong sides together, stitch using a 6 mm (1/4-in) seam allowance. Trim seam allowance to

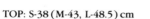

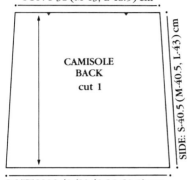

TOP: S-46 (M-51, L-56) cm
CAMISOLE FRONT cut 1
SIDE: S-40.5 (M-40.5, L-43) cm
BOTTOM: S-53.5 (M-58.5, L-63.5) cm

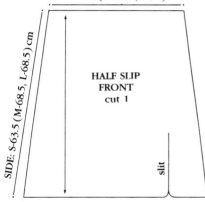

TOP: S-38 (M-43, L-48.5) cm
CAMISOLE BACK cut 1
SIDE: S-40.5 (M-40.5, L-43) cm
BOTTOM: S-43 (M-48.5, L-53.5) cm

(S = Small, M = Medium, L = Large)

3 mm (1/8 in). Turn wrong side out. Stitch 6 mm from first seam, completely enclosing raw edges.

1. Cut camisole front and back from satin. Sew together at sides, using French seams.

2. Baste lace around top edge of right side of camisole. Overlap ends and secure with hand stitches or narrow machine zigzag. With thread to match lace on top and thread to match satin in bobbin, stitch edge of lace to satin, using a narrow machine zigzag. Turn camisole wrong side out. Trim excess satin to within 3 mm (1/8 in) of zigzag stitching line. Remove basting.

3. From satin, cut 2 strips 41 × 2.5 cm (16-1/8 × 1 in), for straps. Cut 2 lengths of string 50 cm (19-3/4 in) long. Fold each strip over a piece of string so right sides are together and long edges meet. Using a 6 mm seam allowance, stitch across one end and up long open edge. Turn straps right side out by pulling string. Cut off strings. Pin straps to camisole at notches on front and back. Try on camisole and check strap length. Adjust to fit if necessary. Stitch straps

in place at top and bottom of lace.

4. Turn under 6 mm then 10 mm (3/8 in) around bottom edge of camisole. Hem.

HALF SLIP

YOU NEED:
- **1.20 m satin, 115 cm wide**
- **1.80 m lace, 125 mm wide**
- **.70 m elastic, 6 mm wide**
- **Matching threads**
- **Brown paper**

TO MAKE:
Draw and cut pattern from brown paper, following measurements for size Small (S), Medium (M) or Large (L) on Diagrams that follow.

1. Cut slip front and back from satin. Sew together at sides, using French seams as described in Camisole instructions (this page).

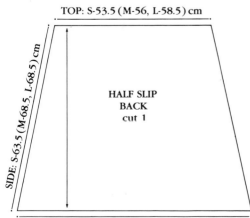

TOP: S-46 (M-48.5, L-51) cm
SIDE: S-63.5 (M-68.5, L-68.5) cm
HALF SLIP FRONT cut 1
slit
BOTTOM: S-66 (M-68.5, L-68.5) cm

TOP: S-53.5 (M-56, L-58.5) cm
SIDE: S-63.5 (M-68.5, L-68.5) cm
HALF SLIP BACK cut 1
BOTTOM: S-78.5 (M-81.5, L-81.5) cm

2. Turn under 6 mm (1/4 in) then 10 mm (3/8 in) around top edge of slip to form casing for elastic. Topstitch close to both folds, leaving a 5 cm (2-in) opening at one side seam. Take waist measurement of wearer and add 3.5 cm (1-3/8 in). Cut a length of elastic to this measurement. Thread elastic through casing. At centre front, smooth out 12.5 cm (5 in) along casing and elastic. Topstitch at each end of this section, through all layers, at right angles to top edge. This will keep the stomach area flat. Overlap ends of elastic 1 cm (3/8 in) and secure with hand stitches. Topstitch

casing opening closed.

3. Starting at top of slit, baste lace to right side of slip, down one edge of slit, around bottom edge (cut and overlap at curves if necessary) and up other edge of slit. Overlap ends and join at top of slit. With thread to match lace on top and thread to match satin in bobbin, stitch edge of lace to satin by hand or using a narrow machine zigzag. Turn slip wrong side out. Trim excess satin to within 3 mm (1/8 in) of stitching line. Remove basting.

4. Trim lace along edges of slit following outline of design motifs.

JEWELRY BOX

YOU NEED:
- **Piece of polyester moiré taffeta, 75 × 40 cm (29-1/2 × 15-3/4 in)**
- **Piece of compressed polyester batting (such as Thermolam), 75 × 40 cm**
- **Matching thread**
- **1 m matching narrow satin cord**
- **.50 m matching satin piping**
- **Oval wooden bead, approx 25 mm long**
- **Pearl bead, 5 mm in diameter**
- **Small amount of crystal rocaille beads**
- **Piece of lightweight cardboard, 38 × 30.5 cm (15 × 12 in)**
- **White craft glue**
- **Fast-bonding "instant" glue**
- **Darning needle**
- **Zipper foot**
- **Brown paper**

TO MAKE:
Draw and cut pattern from brown paper, following measurements on Diagram (at left). Transfer markings.

1. Fold taffeta in half so right sides are together and short edges meet. Place paper pattern on fold. Cut out. Open out taffeta. Baste piping to right side of lid on one half, 1 cm (3/8 in) from edge along dotted line indicated on pattern.

2. Refold taffeta as before so right sides are together. Using a 6 mm (1/4-in) seam allowance, stitch around all edges, leaving open between large dots. Turn right side out.

3. Cut 2 cardboard rectangles and 4 batting rectangles in each of the following sizes: 21 × 5.5 cm (8-1/4 × 2-1/8 in) for front and back; 9 × 5 cm (3-1/2 × 2 in) for sides; 21 × 10 cm (8-1/4 × 4 in) for bottom and lid. (You should have a total of 6 cardboard and 12 batting rectangles.)

4. With white glue, glue a cardboard rectangle between 2 corresponding batting rectangles. Let dry. Insert rectangles into taffeta to check for proper fit. There should be a narrow gap between the rectangles to allow for folding. Remove rectangles to trim if necessary.

5. Firmly push front rectangle into taffeta,

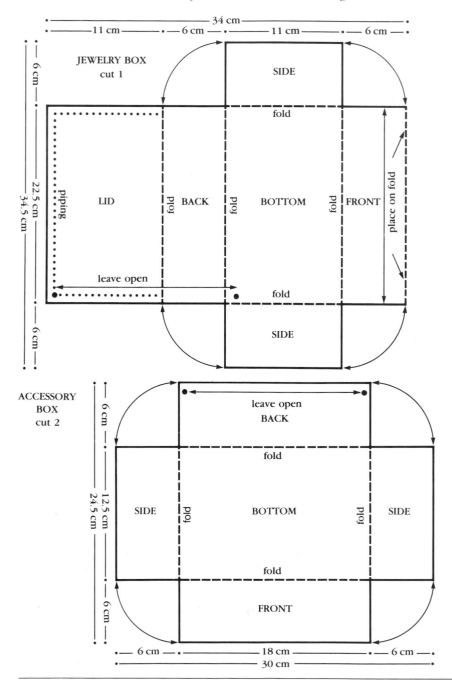

Clockwise from top left: Marbleized Shaker Boxes and Gift Boxes (p. 126), Slipper Pouch and Man's Slippers (p. 127), Cuff Links, (p. 122), Marbleized Gift Tag (p. 126), Bead Necklaces (p. 122), Accessory Box (p. 126) and Cuff Links.

turning all seam allowances to same side (this will be inside of box). Using zipper foot, stitch along fold line, through both layers. Repeat for sides, bottom, back and lid. Turn under 6 mm around opening and slipstitch closed.

6. Fold up sides, front and back as indicated by curved arrows. Using white glue, glue inside edge of corners together. Glue one corner at a time, holding in place with straight pins until glue dries.

7. Cut and set aside a 5 cm (2-in) length of satin cord. Thread one end of remaining length onto darning needle. Glue other end inside wooden bead with fast-bonding glue. Coat outside of bead with white glue. Push needle through

centre hole of bead, around outside of bead and back through hole, repeatedly, until bead is covered with cord. Dab covered bead with fast-bonding glue. Roll in rocaille beads. Glue pearl bead to bottom hole.

8. Loop 5 cm length of cord through one or two cords covering top of bead. Snip a few stitches open at centre front edge of lid. Poke in ends of loop. Slipstitch opening closed, securing cord at same time.

ACCESSORY BOX

YOU NEED:
- **.30 m synthetic suede, 115 cm wide**
- **.30 m compressed polyester batting (such as Thermolam), 115 cm wide**
- **Piece of lightweight cardboard, 53 × 23 cm (20-7/8 × 9 in)**
- **Decoration for lid, such as an old brooch, insignia, initial or blazer crest**
- **Matching thread**
- **White craft glue**
- **Zipper foot**
- **Brown paper**

TO MAKE:
Draw and cut pattern from brown paper, following measurements on Diagram (page 124).
Note: When gluing suede, sponge off any excess glue immediately with warm water.

1. From suede, cut 2 box pieces using paper pattern and 3 lid rectangles as follows: A, 23 × 18.5 cm (9 × 7-1/4 in); B, 18 × 12 cm (7 × 4-3/4 in); C, 18 × 12.5 cm (7 × 5 in). With right sides together and using a 6 mm (1/4-in) seam allowance, stitch 2 box pieces together around all edges, leaving open between large dots. Turn right side out.

2. Cut 2 cardboard rectangles and 4 batting rectangles in each of the following sizes: 16 × 4 cm (6-1/4 × 1-5/8 in) for front and back; 11.5 × 4 cm (4-1/2 × 1-5/8 in) for sides. Cut 1 cardboard and 2 batting rectangles 16 × 11.5 cm for bottom. (You should have a total of 5 cardboard and 10 batting rectangles.)

3. Glue a cardboard rectangle between 2 corresponding batting rectangles. Let

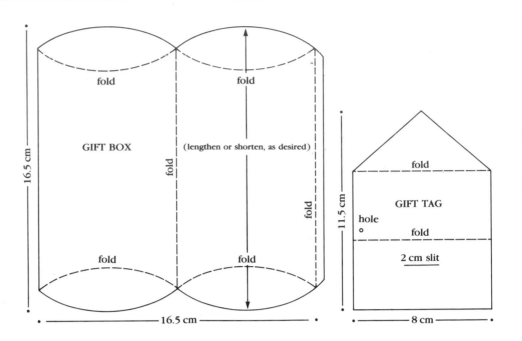

dry. Insert rectangles into suede to check for proper fit. There should be a narrow gap between the rectangles to allow for folding. Remove rectangles to trim if necessary.

4. Firmly push front rectangle into suede. Using zipper foot, stitch along fold line, through both layers. Repeat for sides, bottom and back. Turn under 6 mm around opening and slipstitch closed.

5. Fold up sides, front and back as indicated by curved arrows. Glue inside edge of corners together. Glue one corner at a time, holding in place with straight pins until glue dries.

6. **Lid:** Cut 1 cardboard rectangle and 2 batting rectangles 18.5 × 13.5 cm (7-1/4 × 5-3/8 in). Glue cardboard rectangle between 2 batting rectangles. Centre and glue to wrong side of suede lid rectangle A. Fold under and glue edges of suede to wrong side, mitring at corners. Centre and glue rectangle B to wrong side, covering cardboard. Cut a 15.5 × 10 cm (6-1/8- × 4-in) cardboard rectangle. Centre and glue to wrong side of C. Fold under and glue edges of suede to wrong side, mitring at corners. Centre and glue to wrong side of larger covered lid.

7. Glue decoration to centre front of box lid.

MARBLEIZED SHAKER BOXES, GIFT BOXES AND TAGS

YOU NEED:
- **Small shaker boxes**
- **Lightweight cardboard or Bristol board for gift boxes and tags**
- **Gold spray paint**
- **Small amounts of oil-based paint**
- **Co-ordinating ribbon**
- **Gold cord**
- **Pan (such as an old plastic dishpan)**
- **Newspaper**
- **Stir stick**
- **Utility knife**
- **Hole punch**
- **White craft glue**
- **Brown paper**

TO MARBLEIZE ITEMS:
Cover work area with newspaper. Fill pan with water. Pour in a few drops of oil-based paints and stir gently. Paint swirls will float on the surface. To transfer swirling pattern onto something flat, such as paper or ribbon, place on surface of water and lift off. To transfer onto something that has more depth, grip inside of article with splayed fingers and immerse it in water up to the top edge and lift out. Use a slow, steady down-and-up motion. Place right side up on newspaper. Let dry.

TO MAKE:

MARBLEIZED SHAKER BOX

1. Spray-paint box and lid, inside and out. Let dry.

2. Fill pan with water, 2.5 cm (1 in) deeper than height of box. Add paint and stir. Immerse box. Lift out and place upside down on newspaper to dry. Repeat for lid.

3. Tie lid to box with cord or marbleized ribbon.

GIFT BOX AND TAG

Draw and cut pattern for gift tag and/or box from brown paper, following measurements on Diagrams (at left).

1. Cut box or tag from cardboard. Spray-paint both sides. Let dry.

2. Fill pan with water, add paint and stir. Place one side of cardboard on surface of water. Lift off and let dry, marbleized side up.

3. Score fold lines with scissor blade. Cut slit and punch hole in gift tag. Fold up with marbleized side out. Poke pointed tab into slit to close. Tie loop of cord through hole. Fold gift box in half. Dab glue along narrow flap and glue to inside of box. Fold curved ends in. Tie closed with cord or marbleized ribbon.

MAN'S SLIPPERS

YOU NEED:

- .30 m synthetic suede, 115 cm wide
- **Piece of compressed polyester batting (such as Thermolam), 36 × 22 cm (14-1/4 × 8-5/8 in)**
- **Matching thread**
- **Brown paper**

TO MAKE:

To enlarge slipper pattern, see General Directions (page 134).

1. Fold suede in half so short edges meet. Cut 2 slipper tops, 2 soles for right foot (a top and a bottom), turn pattern piece over and cut 2 soles for left foot. Also cut 2 strips 76 × 3 cm (30 × 1-1/8 in) and 2 strips 25.5 × 3 cm (10 × 1-1/8 in).

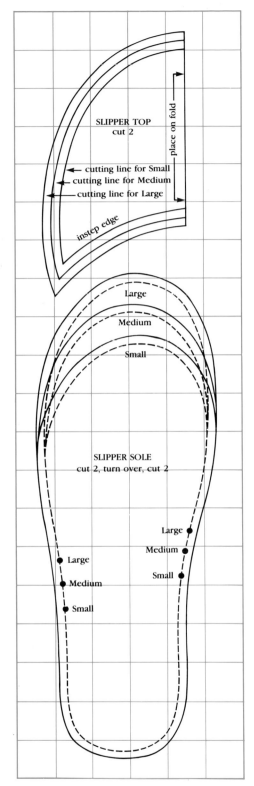

To make pattern for insole, trim 6 mm (1/4 in) off sole pattern piece, as indicated by broken line. Cut 4 insoles from batting.

2. With right sides together and using a 6 mm seam allowance, stitch short strip to instep edge of each slipper top. Fold strip to wrong side forming binding 1 cm (3/8 in) wide. Pin in place from right side. Topstitch along seam line.

3. Sandwich 2 layers of batting between wrong sides of right foot soles. Stitch together 3 mm (1/8 in) from edge. Pin slipper top, right side up, to sole between dots. Baste 3 mm from edge. Repeat for left foot.

4. With right sides together and using a 6 mm seam allowance, stitch long strip around top edge of entire slipper. Fold strip to under side forming binding and topstitch as before.

SLIPPER POUCH

YOU NEED:

- **22 cm synthetic suede, 115 cm wide**
- **Matching zipper, 30.5 cm long**
- **Matching thread**

TO MAKE:

1. From suede, cut 2 rectangles 36.5 × 20.5 cm (14-3/8 × 8 in) and 2 strips 4 × 1 cm (1-5/8 × 3/8 in).

2. With right sides together and using a 13 mm (1/2-in) seam allowance, stitch 2 rectangles together for 3 cm (1-1/8 in) at each end of one long edge. Baste remainder of seam in between. Press seam open. Baste zipper in place on wrong side of seam.

3. Fold one strip in half so wrong sides are together, forming a loop. On right side, pin loop ends to stopper end of zipper, having loop pointing away from zipper. Topstitch zipper in place, catching ends of loop in stitching. Remove basting and open zipper. Thread remaining strip through zipper pull. Fold in half so wrong sides are together and stitch close to pull. Clip ends on the diagonal.

4. With right sides of pouch together and using a 6 mm (1/4-in) seam allowance, stitch around remaining 3 edges. To form box corners, flatten each corner so seams align down the middle. Measure and mark points on each fold, 2 cm (3/4 in) from corner. Stitch across corner from point to point.

ELEGANT EVENING BAG

For that special friend or relative on your Christmas list create a gift she will treasure. Stitched in shades of blue accented with rose and gold and decorated with a gold tassel, it's an unusual little purse to be carried and cherished season after season.

DESIGN BY BEVERLEY McINNES

YOU NEED:

- **No. 13 ecru mono canvas, 2 pieces 23 cm (9 in) square**
- **Piece of lining fabric such as taffeta or medium-weight silky fabric, 46 × 23 cm (18-1/8 × 9 in)**
- **Matching thread**
- **2 skeins each of DMC embroidery floss in shades of blue, No. 791, No. 792, No. 793, No. 794**
- **1 skein each of Marlitt viscose embroidery floss, No. 209 deep rose and No. 019 light rose**
- **11 m DMC Fil Or (gold)**
- **No. 22 tapestry needle**
- **Stretcher frame, 23 cm square (optional)**
- **Masking tape**
- **Metal ring, 5 cm in diameter**
- **20 cm gold chain**
- **Gold tassel**

TO MAKE:

1. Bind edges of canvas pieces with masking tape and staple to frame if using one.

2. Following graph, work repetative design over an area 17 cm (6-3/4 in) long × 13.5 cm (5-1/4 in) wide as follows: First work encroached cross-stitch Xs with all 6 plies of DMC floss (separate plies before threading needle). Work compensating stitches at beginning and end of rows where necessary. Alternate color of pattern repeat, working with 4 shades of blue (e.g. repeat dark to light sequence or work dark to light to dark again, creating a mirror image of colors). Lay horizontal threads of Marlitt viscose floss across Xs over width of work, alternating 8 threads of one color then 8 threads of the other. Couch these threads down with Fil Or where indicated.

Using 5 plies of DMC floss, work 2 rows of continental stitch around edges of entire design. Work second needlepoint panel in same manner.

3. Trim edges of unworked canvas to within 2 cm (3/4 in) of stitched work. Press under all edges of canvas, mitring at corners and leaving 2 rows of mesh along each edge for finishing stitches.

4. Cut 2 rectangles of lining fabric, 1.5 cm (5/8 in) larger than size of pressed needlepoint panels. Press under 1.5 cm on all edges of each piece. Using tiny stitches, slipstitch lining to back of each needlepoint panel, wrong sides together. Be sure the lining does not extend

ELEGANT EVENING BAG

beyond the unworked rows of mesh around edges of panel.

5. Using 4 plies of DMC floss, work herringbone or binding stitch along top edge of each panel. Place front and back panels wrong sides together. Join the panels and finish edges by working binding stitch around sides and bottom.

6. Loop chain through metal ring. With pliers, open link at one end of chain and join to link at other end, forming a complete circle. Sew tassel and one link of chain to side edge of purse approx 5 cm (2 in) from top. To close bag, pleat top edge and push through metal ring.

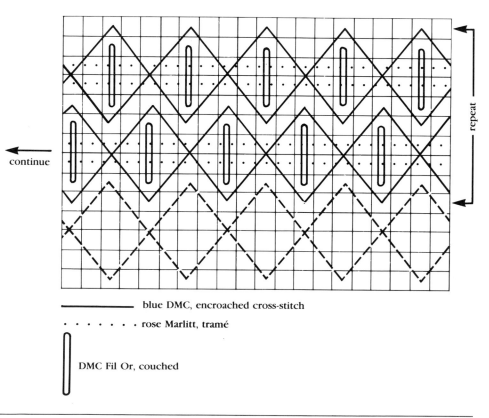

continue ←   repeat

——————— blue DMC, encroached cross-stitch

· · · · · · · rose Marlitt, tramé

▯ DMC Fil Or, couched

WILD ROSE WOOD CARVING

Hand-carving is a time-honored tradition that can turn the most practical items into gifts of beauty. The carved motif in this breadboard and shelf is a stylized Canadian wild rose, found in fields from Quebec to the Yukon in summertime.

DESIGNS BY JO CALVERT

YOU NEED:

For both projects:

- X-acto knife or utility knife
- 2 carving tools approx 3 mm (1/8 in) deep, one a sharp V-shape and the other a shallow crescent shape
- Soft pencil
- Fine sandpaper
- Tracing paper

For breadboard:

- Hardwood breadboard
- Mineral oil and rag

For shelf:

- 3-ft length of 1- × 6-in hardwood
- 2, 2-in wood screws
- 2, 1-in wood screws
- Drill with bits to correspond to screws

- Jigsaw
- Clamps
- Screwdriver
- Carpenter's glue
- Varnish or wax
- Brown paper

BREADBOARD

TO TRANSFER DESIGN (*shown actual size on page 142*):

Trace solid lines of wild rose motif onto tracing paper with soft pencil. Turn paper over. Retrace lines on reverse side. Place paper right side up on right side of board, keeping design at least 1.5 cm (5/8 in)

from edges of board. Firmly redraw over lines of design, using just enough pressure to transfer lines onto wood.

TO CARVE:

Note: Be sure to carve away from yourself, turning board when necessary. Work slowly, rocking blade slightly as you carve. To prevent chipped edges, always carve towards a cut edge. Carved areas should slope towards centre of design. If carving becomes deeper than depth of vertical cuts along outlines, recut outlines with knife to preserve a clean edge.

1. With knife, make a vertical cut at least 3 mm (1/8 in) deep along all solid lines

of design. These cuts act as a guide for the carving tools and prevent the blade from slipping.

2. Using V tool, carve along all cut lines. Using crescent tool, carve out all areas of petals indicated by dots. Carve towards centre of flower, stopping at cut line. Also with crescent tool, carve out interior of each leaf indicated by dots, stopping at cut line around edge of petals. Using V tool, carve a vein line on each leaf. Finally, using crescent tool and carving towards centre, carve around all edges of flower and leaves where indicated by dots.

3. Using V tool, carve a line around inside edge of breadboard.

4. Sand finished board and carved areas lightly. Rub with mineral oil (do not use furniture oil as this can be toxic).

SHELF

TO MAKE:

To enlarge diagram/pattern, see General Directions (page 134).

1. Trace outline of shelf, brace and 2 supports onto wood following diagram layout. Cut out.

2. Drill holes to fit long screws 1-1/4 inches in from each end of front surface of brace. Having back edges flush, fit top surface of brace against underside of shelf as indicated by broken lines on Diagram. From underside of brace, drill 1-in-deep holes (through brace and part way into shelf) to fit shorter screws, 2 inches in from each end.

3. Positioning motif as shown, transfer

wild rose motif onto one side of one shelf support as given in Breadboard instructions. Turn tracing paper over and transfer reversed design onto opposite side of other shelf support (each support should be a mirror image of the other).

4. Carve designs as for Breadboard, Steps 1 to 3.

5. Round and sand edges of shelf and shelf support. Sand carved areas lightly.

6. Glue and screw brace to underside of shelf. Having back and front edges flush and carved designs facing outward, glue top edge of shelf supports to underside of shelf where indicated by broken lines. Clamp. Let dry.

7. Lightly sand assembled shelf. Wax or varnish as desired. Attach shelf to wall with 2 long screws.

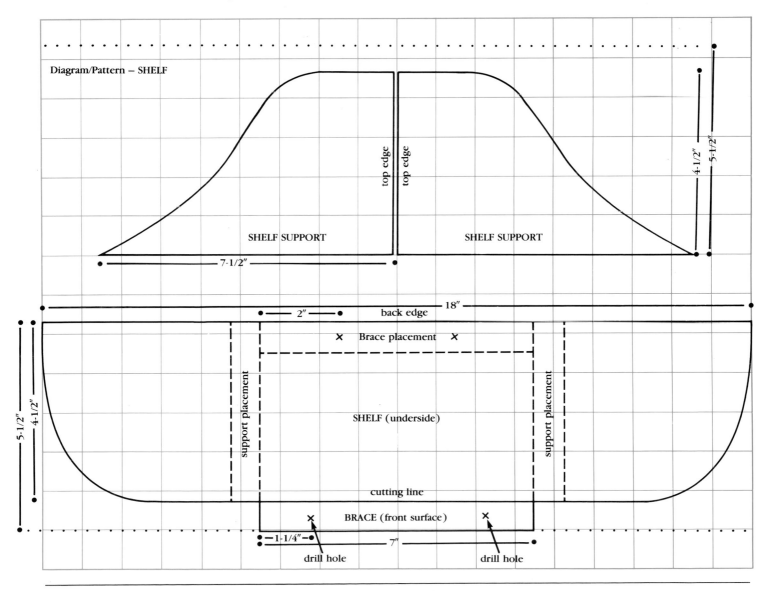

Diagram/Pattern — SHELF

SHELF SUPPORT   SHELF SUPPORT

4-1/2"   5-1/2"

7-1/2"

18"

2"   back edge

Brace placement

support placement   support placement

5-1/2"   4-1/2"

SHELF (underside)

cutting line

BRACE (front surface)

1-1/4"   7"

drill hole   drill hole

TROMPE L'OEIL WINDOW

Some gifts can't be bought at any price — especially ones handcrafted with a special person in mind. For the executive in a windowless office, make a Trompe l'Oeil Window and turn his or her work space into a unique room with a view.

DESIGN BY JANE BUCKLES

YOU NEED:
- Piece of 3/8-in plywood, good on one side, 21-1/2 × 30-3/4 in
- Piece of 1- × 4-in* pine, 90 in long
- Piece of 1- × 5-in* pine, 45 in long
- Scraps of 1-in pine, approx 14 × 7 in, for pot and tulips
- Strip of cove or quarter-round molding, 22 in long
- 3/8-in dowelling, 15 in long
- Drill with 3/8-in bit and bit to correspond to size of screws
- 1-in screws
- 1-1/4-in spiral finishing nails
- 2 screw eyes
- Picture frame wire
- Hammer
- Saw
- Jigsaw
- X-acto knife
- Sandpaper
- White craft glue

- White primer paint
- Acrylic or oil-based paint, colors as desired
- Paintbrushes
- Brown paper

*These measurements are nominal sizes quoted by lumber industry. Actual size is generally 1/2 to 3/4 in less.

TO MAKE:

To enlarge window scene and flowerpot patterns, see General Directions (page 134).

1. From 1- × 4-in pine, cut 2 pieces each 22-1/2 in long and 1 piece 22 in long for window frame. From 1- × 5-in pine, cut 1 piece 22 in long and another piece 23 in long for windowsill. Lightly sand these pieces as well as plywood rectangle and molding.

2. Paint molding, frame and sill pieces in desired color. Paint good side of plywood with primer. Let dry. Transfer enlarged outdoor scene or draw your own scene on primed plywood. Paint as desired or use photo as a guide. Paint or stencil small details such as sheep in foreground, blind pull and snowflakes.

3. Trace pattern for flowerpot and 2 tulips onto scraps of 1-in pine. Cut out with a jigsaw. From dowelling, cut stems 6-1/2 in long and 5 in long and two 1-1/4-in dowel pins. Paint flowerpot, tulips and stems. Let dry.
Drill a 3/8-in hole in bottom of each flower. Glue and insert stems. Drill similar holes in top of flowerpot, approx 3 in apart. Glue and insert stems.

4. Drill two 3/8-in holes in bottom of flowerpot. Glue and insert dowel pins.

5. Centre and nail 23-in length of 1- × 5-in pine at right angles to and onto top edge of 22-in piece to form windowsill (see Diagram).

6. Referring to Diagram, assemble remaining pieces to form a frame around painted side of plywood, so frame overlaps approx 1/4 in over edge of plywood. Screw pieces securely in place from back of window. Glue molding in place under sill.

7. Drill two 3/8-in holes in windowsill to take dowel pins on bottom of flowerpot. Insert flowerpot. Do *not* glue. Wooden pot may be replaced by a real pot of flowers when desired.

8. Insert screw eyes into either side of back of window. String picture wire between 2 eyes to hang.

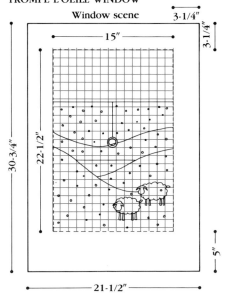

TROMPE L'OEILE WINDOW
Window scene

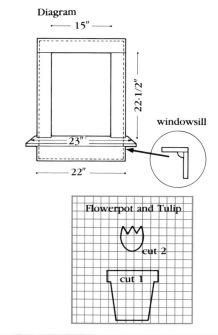

Diagram

windowsill

Flowerpot and Tulip

cut 2

cut 1

GENERAL DIRECTIONS

TO ENLARGE PATTERN

Enlarge pattern by the squaring method, as follows: On brown paper, draw a grid of horizontal and vertical lines 2.5 cm (1 in) apart. Each square on the diagram equals a 2.5 cm square on your paper. Enlarge by drawing each line of the design onto the corresponding square on your paper. Transfer any markings.

TO TRANSFER PATTERN

There are several methods of transferring a pattern. Choose the one best suited to the pattern and materials used.

Carbon paper or dressmaker's carbon

Use carbon paper for paper and cardboard projects only. Use dressmaker's carbon for fabric, in a color close to that of the fabric. Place carbon face down on fabric. Place pattern on top. With tracing wheel or pencil, draw over pattern, using just enough pressure to transfer lines.

Soft pencil

Use on wood or cardboard. Using soft pencil, trace pattern onto tracing paper. Turn paper over. Retrace lines on reverse side. Place paper right side up on wood or cardboard. Firmly redraw pattern, using just enough pressure to transfer lines.

Basting

To transfer pattern to dark, soft, heavily textured, stretchy or sheer fabrics, trace pattern onto tissue paper. Pin to fabric. Hand- or machine-baste around lines. Tear away tissue. When work is complete, remove basting.

Water-soluble marking pen

Use on needlepoint canvas and sheer washable fabrics. With pattern under canvas or fabric, lightly trace design onto right side. To remove markings, dampen fabric, and drawn lines will disappear.

KNITTING AND CROCHET ABBREVIATIONS

beg	=	begin(ning)
CC	=	contrasting color
ch	=	chain
cm	=	centimetre(s)
dc	=	double crochet
dec	=	decrease(s) (d) (ing)
g	=	gram(s)
inc	=	increase(s) (d) (ing)
in(s)	=	inch(es)
k	=	knit
lp(s)	=	loop(s)
Ml	=	make 1 stitch by picking up horizontal loop in front of next stitch and knitting into back of it
MC	=	main color
mm	=	millimetre(s)
p	=	purl
psso	=	pass slip stitch(es) over
rem	=	remain(ing)
rep	=	repeat(ed) (ing)
rnd(s)	=	round(s)
sc	=	single crochet
sk	=	skip
sl	=	slip
sl st	=	slip stitch
sp(s)	=	space(s)
st(s)	=	stitch(es)
St st	=	stocking stitch
tbl	=	through back of loop
tog	=	together

Simplified Instructions (Simplified Instructions)

All knitting and crochet instructions that appear in this book conform to national knitting and crochet standards.

TENSION

It is essential to work to the exact tension with the specified yarn to obtain satisfactory results. Before beginning any knitting or crochet project, make a test swatch at least 10 cm (4 ins) square using the specified yarn, needles or hook and stitch pattern. Individual knitting and crochet tension may vary, so it may be necessary to adjust needle or hook size to achieve the tension given. TO SAVE TIME, TAKE TIME TO CHECK TENSION.

FULL-SIZE PATTERNS

The full-size patterns appearing on the following pages can be traced or photocopied for use with the corresponding instructions found in the main body of this book.

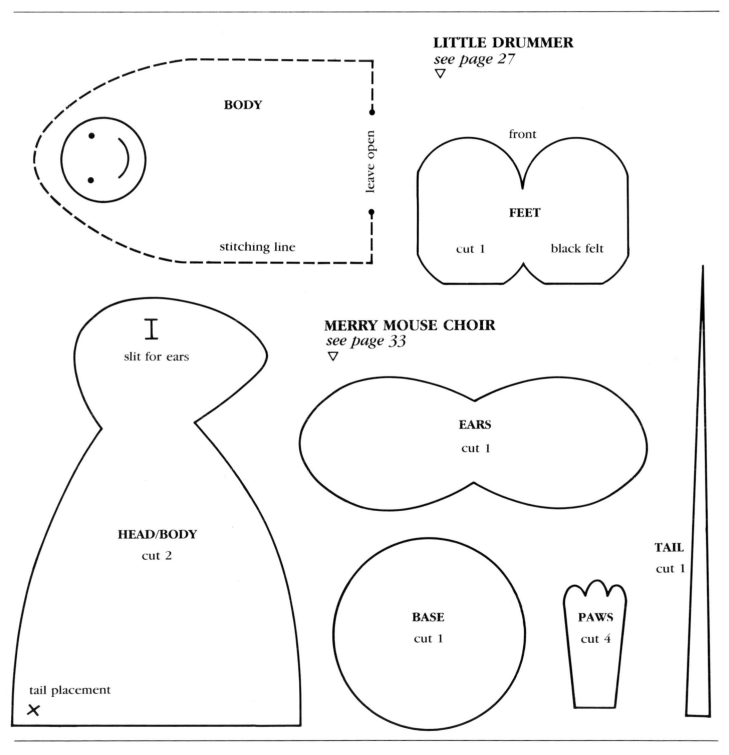

LITTLE DRUMMER
see page 27
▽

BODY

leave open

stitching line

front

FEET

cut 1   black felt

MERRY MOUSE CHOIR
see page 33
▽

slit for ears

EARS

cut 1

HEAD/BODY

cut 2

BASE

cut 1

PAWS

cut 4

TAIL

cut 1

tail placement

✗

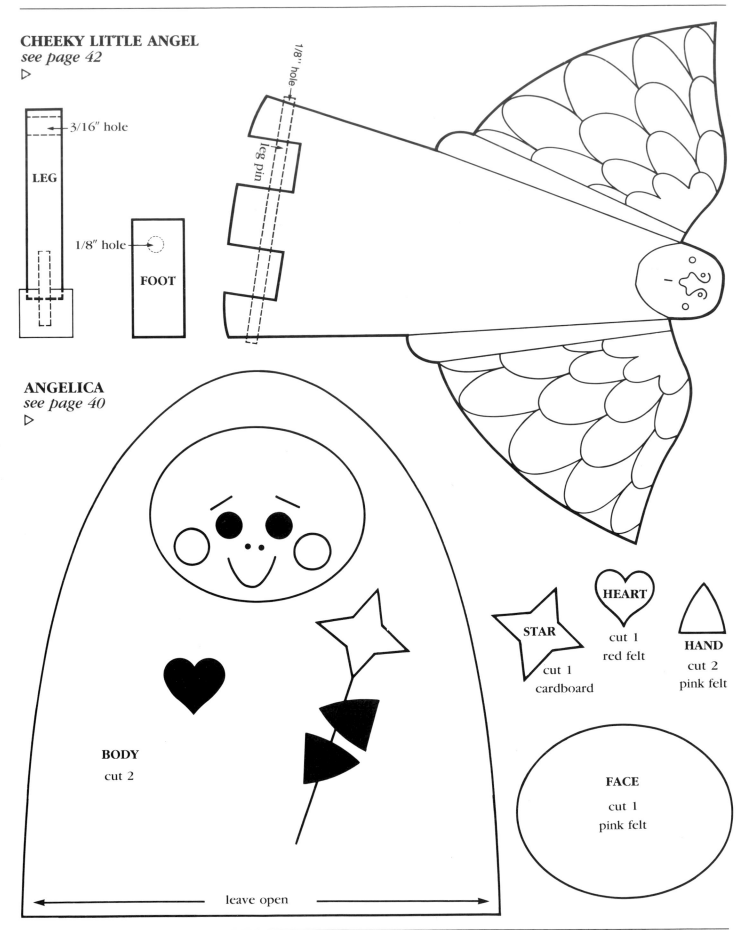

CHEEKY LITTLE ANGEL
see page 42
▷

3/16″ hole

LEG

1/8″ hole

FOOT

1/8″ hole

leg pin

ANGELICA
see page 40
▷

BODY

cut 2

leave open

HEART

cut 1
red felt

STAR

cut 1
cardboard

HAND

cut 2
pink felt

FACE

cut 1
pink felt

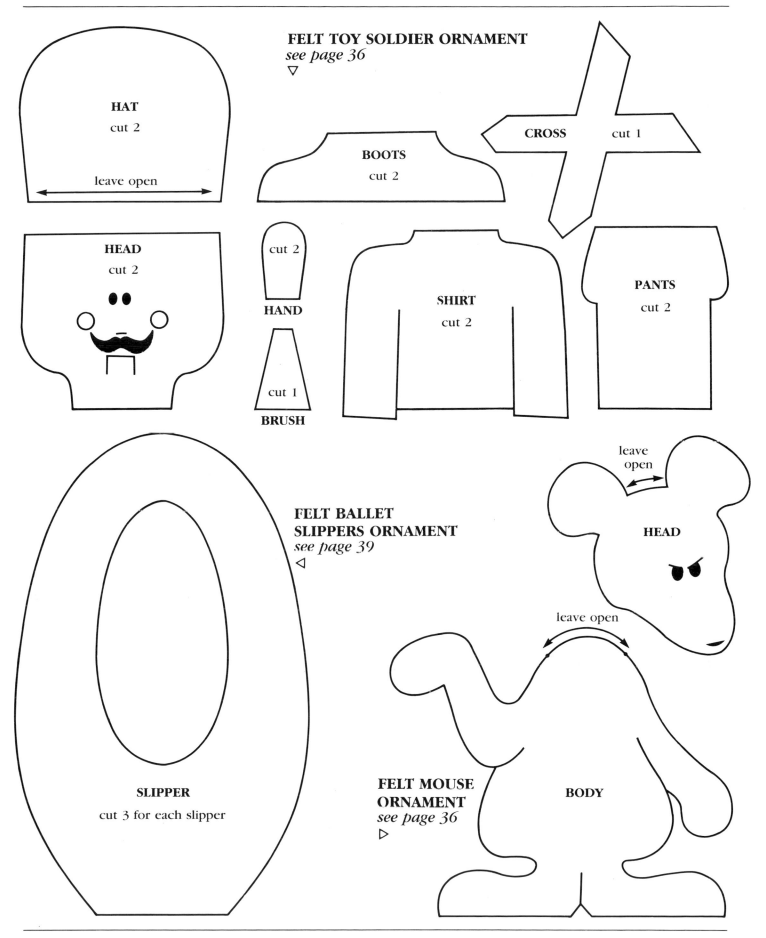

FELT TOY SOLDIER ORNAMENT
see page 36
▽

HAT
cut 2

leave open

BOOTS
cut 2

CROSS   cut 1

HEAD
cut 2

cut 2

HAND

SHIRT
cut 2

PANTS
cut 2

cut 1

BRUSH

leave open

HEAD

**FELT BALLET
SLIPPERS ORNAMENT**
see page 39
◁

leave open

SLIPPER
cut 3 for each slipper

**FELT MOUSE
ORNAMENT**
see page 36
▷

BODY

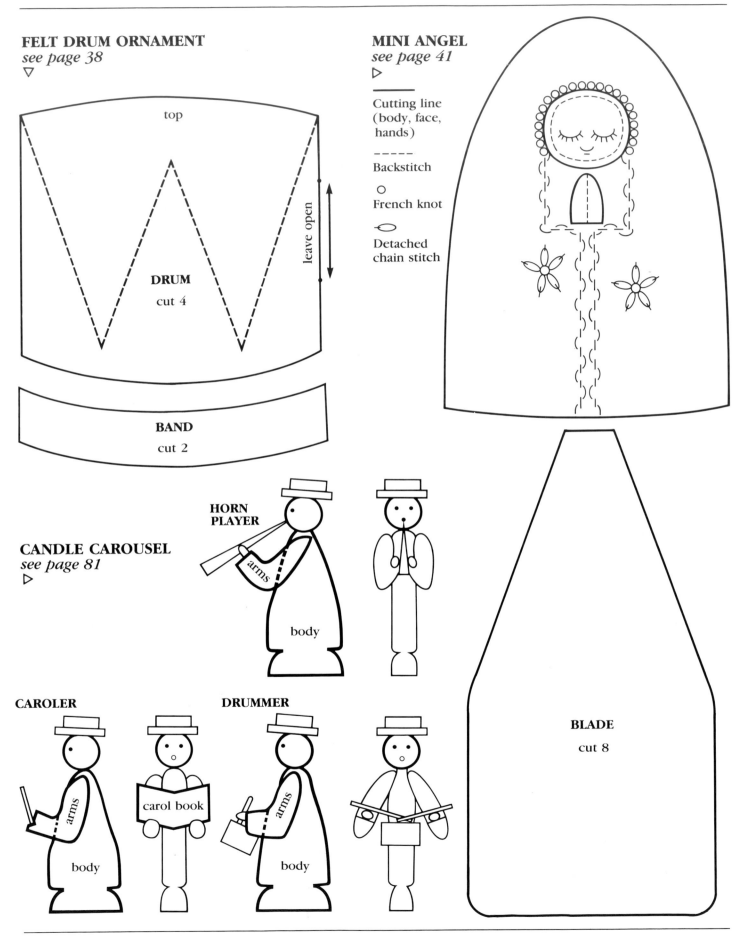

FELT DRUM ORNAMENT
see page 38
▽

top

DRUM

cut 4

leave open

BAND

cut 2

MINI ANGEL
see page 41
▷

——— Cutting line (body, face, hands)

----- Backstitch

○ French knot

⬭ Detached chain stitch

CANDLE CAROUSEL
see page 81
▷

HORN PLAYER

arms

body

CAROLER

arms

body

carol book

DRUMMER

arms

body

BLADE

cut 8

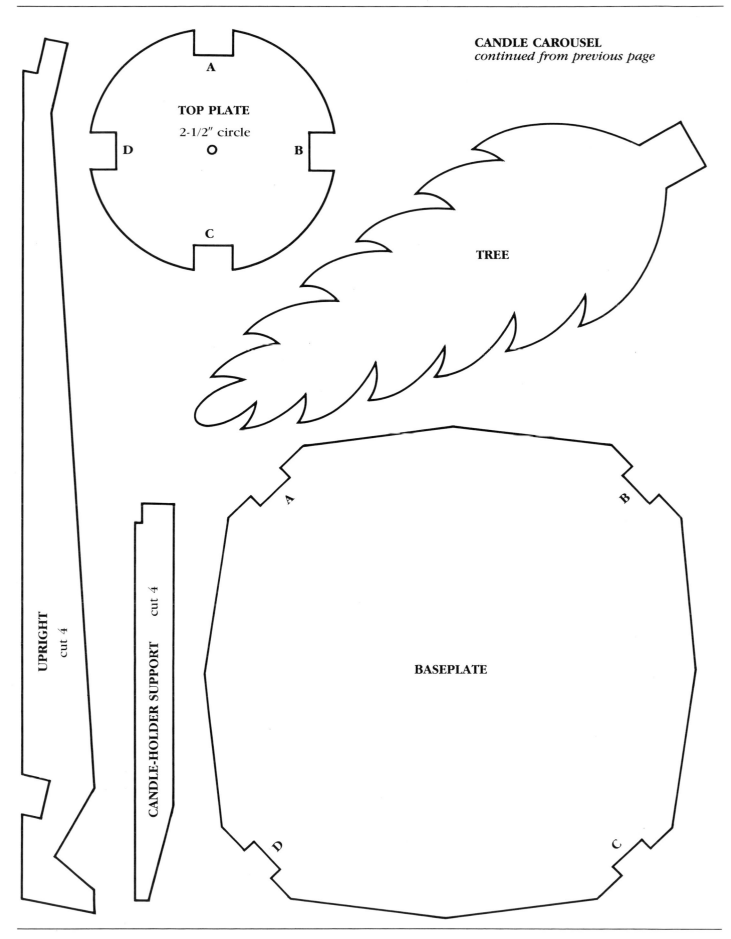

CANDLE CAROUSEL
continued from previous page

TOP PLATE

2-1/2″ circle

A

D   O   B

C

TREE

UPRIGHT
cut 4

CANDLE-HOLDER SUPPORT   cut 4

BASEPLATE

A   B

D   C

MR. AND MRS. CLAUS
see page 101
▽

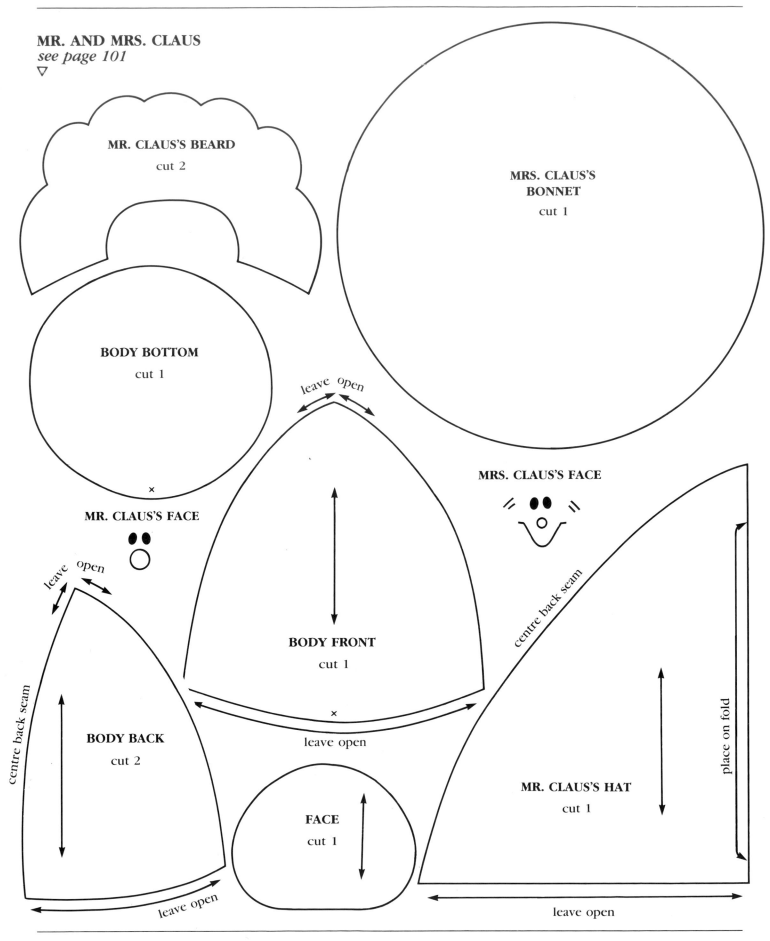

MR. CLAUS'S BEARD
cut 2

MRS. CLAUS'S
BONNET
cut 1

BODY BOTTOM
cut 1

leave open

MRS. CLAUS'S FACE

MR. CLAUS'S FACE

leave open

centre back seam

BODY FRONT
cut 1

leave open

centre back seam

place on fold

BODY BACK
cut 2

leave open

FACE
cut 1

MR. CLAUS'S HAT
cut 1

leave open

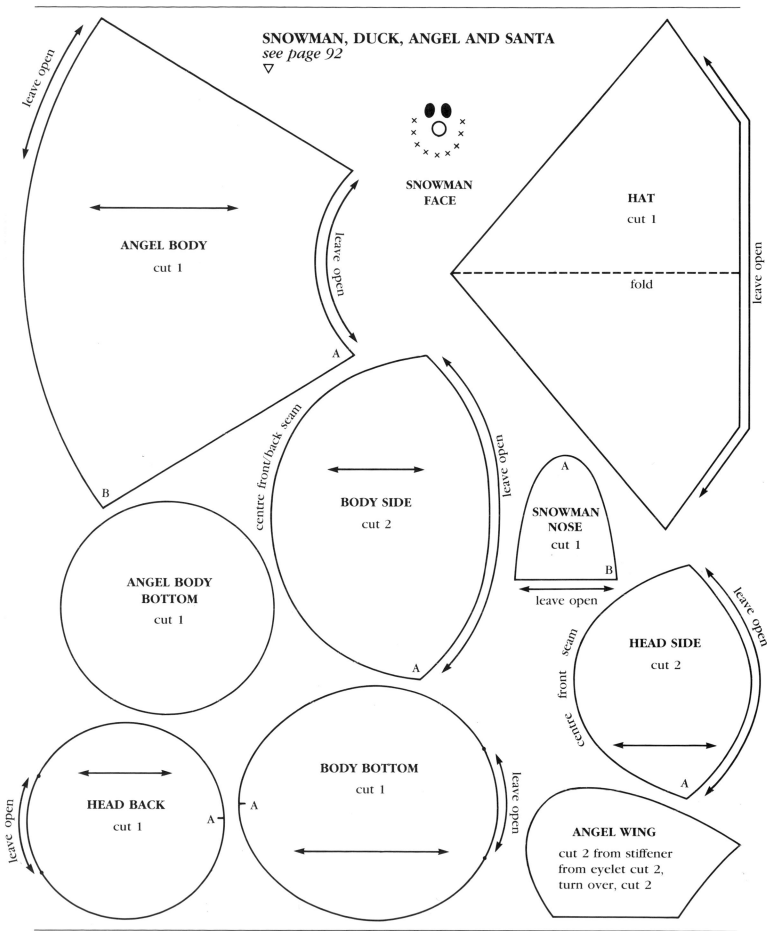

SNOWMAN, DUCK, ANGEL AND SANTA
see page 92

SNOWMAN
FACE

HAT
cut 1

fold

leave open

ANGEL BODY

cut 1

leave open

leave open

A

B

centre front/back seam

BODY SIDE

cut 2

leave open

A

SNOWMAN
NOSE

cut 1

A

B

leave open

ANGEL BODY
BOTTOM

cut 1

leave open

HEAD SIDE

cut 2

centre front seam

A

HEAD BACK

cut 1

A

A

BODY BOTTOM

cut 1

leave open

leave open

ANGEL WING

cut 2 from stiffener
from eyelet cut 2,
turn over, cut 2

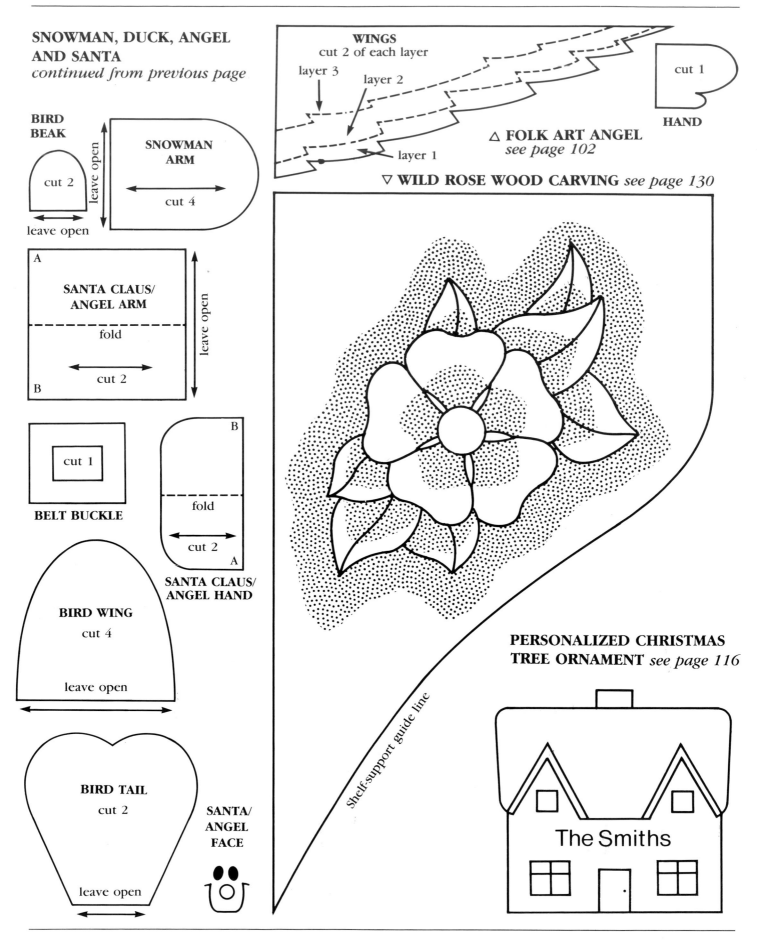

**SNOWMAN, DUCK, ANGEL
AND SANTA**
continued from previous page

WINGS
cut 2 of each layer
layer 3
layer 2
layer 1

cut 1

HAND

△ **FOLK ART ANGEL**
see page 102

▽ **WILD ROSE WOOD CARVING** *see page 130*

**BIRD
BEAK**

cut 2

leave open
leave open

**SNOWMAN
ARM**

cut 4

A

**SANTA CLAUS/
ANGEL ARM**

fold

cut 2

leave open

B

cut 1

BELT BUCKLE

B

fold

cut 2

A

**SANTA CLAUS/
ANGEL HAND**

BIRD WING

cut 4

leave open

BIRD TAIL

cut 2

leave open

**SANTA/
ANGEL
FACE**

Shelf-support guide line

**PERSONALIZED CHRISTMAS
TREE ORNAMENT** *see page 116*

The Smiths

ACKNOWLEDGMENTS AND CREDITS

THE CONTRIBUTORS

Ann Bouffard is an expert at making elaborate bread dough ornaments. For the Inuit ornaments she took her craft to the simplest form, proving that simplest is often best . . . **Jane Buckles,** a former art teacher, now designs full time. Her fabric mâché and wood pieces have been shown in galleries across Canada and the United States . . . Designer **Jo Calvert** works magic with her sewing machine specializing in patchwork, machine-appliqué and embroidery. Her talents also extend to woodworking (see pages 130-131) . . . **Louise Chisholm,** a Nova Scotia craftswoman, has the distinction of designing one of the tiniest items in this book, Angel Fluff . . . As the crafts featured in A Toy Soldier Story and Festive Roller Printing convey, **Mary Corcoran** enjoys creating figures that are whimsical and fun to make. The Christmas craft workshops she conducts at her Ontario farmhouse are a perennial favorite . . . Angelica is an adorable little ornament which comes to us from **Joan Doherty** of Halifax, Nova Scotia. Joan's specialty is doll making for collections . . . **Denise Flys,** owner of Mostly Dolls, a shop in Toronto, has been contributing doll and costume designs to *Canadian Living* since 1978 . . . **Hugh Hope**'s Candle Carousel was inspired by an authentic German carousel he and his family have displayed for many Christmases . . . **Randy Lancaster**'s craft medium is glass as reflected in the lovely Stained Glass Manger Scene on page 79. Randy lives in West Vancouver, British Columbia and has been designing for the past eight years . . . **Christine McCormack,** whose

jolly Elf is on page 99, gets much pleasure and satisfaction in custom designing crafts for special groups such as the elderly and mentally handicapped . . . **Beverley McInnes** of Halifax is a talented needlewoman and teacher. Her beautiful Elegant Evening Bag is on page 129 . . . As a kindergarten teacher, **Sally Medland** thoroughly enjoys developing projects for youngsters. The crafts from Gifts For Little Hands To Make have provided hours of fun for her classes, not to mention her two young sons . . . The glorious choir girls that grace our cover come to us from **Carol Moore**. Carol is the owner of a gift store in White Rock, British Columbia called The Country Wreath . . . **Joan Phillips** has been associated with *Canadian Living* since its early years. The classes given at her Oakville, Ontario shop, The Silver Thimble Inc., provide an excellent sounding board for new ideas and trends . . . Winnipeg doll maker **Judy Pilgrim Stewart,** whose old-fashioned doll, Emma, is featured in this book, is a museum curator specializing in historic costume and textiles . . . **Beverley Plaxton,** a multi-talented Torontonian who designed the My Twin Doll, now specializes in portrait photography . . . The exquisite Treetop Angel and its miniature version are indicative of **Carol Schmidt**'s intricate and beautiful needle-work . . . Several of **Renée Schwarz**'s outstanding designs appear in this book. Specializing in children's clothing, accessories and toys, her work has been featured in *Better Homes and Gardens* and *Woman's Day* magazines . . . **Jean Scobie** is assistant craft editor at *Canadian Living* and a regular

contributor of craft designs. Knitwear design is her first love, but her experience and interest in crafts is broad-ranging . . . **Norene Smiley**'s whimsical Finger Puppets are examples of the craft area she enjoys most — soft toys and puppets . . . **Carolyn Smith** has proven her varied talents with designs such as the Merry Mouse Choir and those for Luxurious Gifts. Doll making is her greatest area of interest . . . The creator of the Santa and Mrs. Claus heirloom figures, **Margaret Stephenson Coole**'s specialties are quilted wall hangings and embroideries. Her work has been exhibited throughout the United States, Canada and overseas . . . Before she retired, **Sister Catherine Mary Strong**, O.S.U., spent many years teaching young children, nurturing their creative abilities with projects such as Saucy Santas pictured on page 47 . . .

PHOTOGRAPHY CREDITS

Chris Campbell: pages 34, 35, 44, 47, 108.
Greg Eligh: pages 26, 28, 29, 31, 32, 116 – 18 (top), 119.
Frank Grant: pages 5 (top left), 8 – 10, 12 – 19, 21, 22, 33, 77, 81, 103 – 5, 107, 110, 118 (bottom).
Sherman Hines: pages 66, 67, 69, 79.
John Stephens: jacket front, pages 2, 3, 5 (bottom left, centre, and right), 24, 37 – 39, 41 – 43, 46, 48 – 51, 53 – 58, 60, 61, 63 – 65, 71, 75, 84, 86 – 88, 90 – 101, 113 – 15, 120, 121, 125, 129, 130, 133.
Maynard Switzer: page 40.

Pattern and Diagram Artwork: Montecolour Ltd.

INDEX

DESIGN AND ART DIRECTION: Gordon Sibley Design Inc.
EDITORIAL: Hugh Brewster
Catherine Fraccaro
PRODUCTION: Susan Barrable
Pamela Yong
TYPOGRAPHY: Q-Composition Inc.
JACKET FILM SEPARATION: Colour Technologies
COLOR SEPARATION,
PRINTING AND BINDING: New Interlitho S.p.A.

CANADIAN LIVING
ADVISORY BOARD: Robert A. Murray
Judy Brandow
Anna Hobbs
Jennifer MacMillan
Jean Scobie

GLORIOUS CHRISTMAS CRAFTS was
produced by Madison Press Books under
the direction of A.E. Cummings.